Achieving Global Food Security
The Caribbean Experience and Beyond

Achieving Global Food Security
The Caribbean Experience and Beyond

Mohamed Irfaan Ali

World Scientific

NEW JERSEY · LONDON · SINGAPORE · BEIJING · SHANGHAI · HONG KONG · TAIPEI · CHENNAI · TOKYO

Published by

World Scientific Publishing Co. Pte. Ltd.
5 Toh Tuck Link, Singapore 596224
USA office: 27 Warren Street, Suite 401-402, Hackensack, NJ 07601
UK office: 57 Shelton Street, Covent Garden, London WC2H 9HE

Library of Congress Cataloging-in-Publication Data
Names: Ali, Mohamed Irfaan, author.
Title: Achieving global food security : the Caribbean experience and beyond / Mohamed Irfaan Ali.
Description: New Hersey : World Scientific, [2025] | Includes bibliographical references and index.
Identifiers: LCCN 2024033909 (print) | LCCN 2024033910 (ebook) |
  ISBN 9789811298899 (hardback) | ISBN 9789811298905 (ebook)|
  ISBN 9789811298912
Subjects: LCSH: Food security--Caribbean Region. | Food supply--Government policy--
  Caribbean Region. | Food security.
Classification: LCC HD9018.C27 A45 2025 (print) | LCC HD9018.C27 (ebook) |
  DDC 338.1/9729--dc23/eng/20240725
LC record available at https://lccn.loc.gov/2024033909
LC ebook record available at https://lccn.loc.gov/2024033910

British Library Cataloguing-in-Publication Data
A catalogue record for this book is available from the British Library.

Copyright © 2025 by World Scientific Publishing Co. Pte. Ltd.

All rights reserved. This book, or parts thereof, may not be reproduced in any form or by any means, electronic or mechanical, including photocopying, recording or any information storage and retrieval system now known or to be invented, without written permission from the publisher.

For photocopying of material in this volume, please pay a copying fee through the Copyright Clearance Center, Inc., 222 Rosewood Drive, Danvers, MA 01923, USA. In this case permission to photocopy is not required from the publisher.

For any available supplementary material, please visit
https://www.worldscientific.com/worldscibooks/10.1142/14005#t=suppl

Desk Editor: Kura Sunaina

Typeset by Stallion Press
Email: enquiries@stallionpress.com

Contents

Acronyms ... ix

About the Author ... xi

Author's Note ... xiii

Message I ... xv

Message II ... xvii

Preface
    Introduction: A Vital Blueprint for Food and Human Security in the 21st Century ... xxi

Chapter 1 Introduction ... 1

Chapter 2 The Global Picture: Food Security — Challenges and Limitations ... 3
  2.1. Inflation ... 4
  2.2. War in Ukraine ... 5
  2.3. COVID-19 Pandemic ... 6
  2.4. Climate Change ... 7
  2.5. Logistics and Supply Chain Crisis ... 7
  2.6. The Global Energy Crisis ... 8

Chapter 3 The Regional Picture ... 11
  3.1. Food Imports ... 11
  3.2. Macroeconomic Overview ... 14
      3.2.1. Private sector investment in agriculture ... 16

3.2.2. Inflation and public debt	17
3.2.3. Climate change	20
Chapter 4 Country Briefs	**23**
4.1. Antigua and Barbuda	23
4.1.1. Overview of the agricultural sector in Antigua and Barbuda	24
4.1.2. Impact of climate change on Antigua and Barbuda's food production	24
4.1.3. Food production in Antigua and Barbuda	25
4.1.4. Investment in agriculture and public debt	26
4.2. The Bahamas	27
4.2.1. Overview of the agricultural sector in the Bahamas	28
4.2.2. Impact of climate change on the Bahamas' food production	28
4.2.3. Food imports dependency	29
4.2.4. Public debt	29
4.3. Barbados	31
4.3.1. Overview of the agricultural sector of Barbados	31
4.3.2. Impact of climate change on food production	32
4.3.3. Investment in agriculture and public debt	33
4.4. Belize	34
4.4.1. Overview of the agricultural sector of Belize	35
4.4.2. Impact of climate change on food production	36
4.5. Dominica	38
4.5.1. Overview of the agricultural sector of Dominica	38
4.5.2. Impact of climate change on food production	39
4.5.3. Food import dependency	39
4.5.4. Investment in agriculture and public debt	40
4.6. Grenada	41
4.6.1. Overview of the agricultural sector of Grenada	42
4.6.2. Impact of climate change on food production	42
4.6.3. Food import dependency	43
4.6.4. Investment in agriculture and public debt	43

4.7.	Guyana		45
	4.7.1.	Overview of the agricultural sector of Guyana	46
	4.7.2.	Impact of climate change on food production	46
	4.7.3.	Food import dependency	47
	4.7.4.	Investment in agriculture and public debt	48
4.8.	Haiti		49
	4.8.1.	Overview of the agricultural sector	50
	4.8.2.	Impact of climate change on food production	50
	4.8.3.	Food import dependency	51
	4.8.4.	Investment in agriculture and public debt	53
4.9.	Jamaica		54
	4.9.1.	Overview of the agricultural sector	54
	4.9.2.	Impact of climate change on food production	55
	4.9.3.	Food imports dependency	55
4.10.	Saint Lucia		57
	4.10.1.	Overview of the agricultural sector	58
	4.10.2.	Impact of climate change on food production	58
	4.10.3.	Food import dependency	59
	4.10.4.	Investment in agriculture and public debt	60
4.11.	Saint Kitts and Nevis		62
	4.11.1.	Overview of the agricultural sector	62
	4.11.2.	Impact of climate change on food production	63
	4.11.3.	Food import dependency	64
4.12.	Saint Vincent and the Grenadines		66
	4.12.1.	Overview of the agricultural sector	66
	4.12.2.	Impact of climate change on food production	67
	4.12.3.	Food import dependency	68
	4.12.4.	Investment in agriculture and public debt	69
4.13.	Suriname		70
	4.13.1.	Overview of the agricultural sector	71
	4.13.2.	Impact of climate change on food production	71
	4.13.3.	Food import dependency	72
	4.13.4.	Agricultural investment by the private sector and public debt	73
4.14.	Trinidad and Tobago		75
	4.14.1.	Overview of the agricultural sector	76

viii *Achieving Global Food Security: The Caribbean Experience and Beyond*

4.14.2. Impact of climate change on food production	76
4.14.3. Food import dependency	76
4.14.4. Investment in agriculture and public debt	79

Chapter 5 Strategic Policy Recommendations — **81**

5.1. Establishment of a Regional Agro-Tech Campus	82
5.2. Roraima as an Alternative Food Supplier	89
5.3. Commercialisation of Food Supply	92
5.3.1. E-Agriculture	92
5.4. Caricom Cross Border Agri-Food Investment Strategy	94
5.4.1. Removal of non-tariff barriers to trade	95
5.4.2. De-risking of the agricultural sector	96
5.4.3. Improving transportation and logistics regionally	97
5.4.4. Removal of technical barriers	98
5.4.5. Investment in production, research and development	99

Chapter 6 Works in the Pipeline and Way Forward: Guyana — **101**

6.1. Corn and Soya Bean Pilot Project	101
6.2. Bilateral Partnership to Advance Agriculture	102
6.3. Building a Regional Food Hub	104
6.4. Regional Aquaculture Potential and How We Can Become a Net Global Supplier	105
6.5. Future of Horticulture and Livestock in Guyana	106
6.5.1. Horticulture	107
6.5.2. Livestock	107
6.6. Investment in Agro-processing	108
6.7. Low Carbon Development Strategy	108
6.8. Agriculture Tourism, IWRM, and Land Tenure	110
6.8.1. Policy recommendations	110

Bibliography	113
Name Index	123
Subject Index	125

Acronyms

BBC	Bangalore Bioinnovation Centre
CAHFSA	Caribbean Agricultural Health and Food Safety Agency
CARDI	Caribbean Agricultural Research and Development Institute
CARICOM	Caribbean Community
CDB	Caribbean Development Bank
CELAC	Community of Latin American and Caribbean States
CET	Common External Tariff
CPI	Consumer Price Index
CPSO	Caribbean Private Sector Organization
ECLAC	United Nations Economic Commission for Latin America and the Caribbean
EDF	European Development Fund
FAO	The Food and Agriculture Organization of the United Nations
GCF	Green Climate Fund
GDP	Gross Domestic Product
GFDRR	Global Facility for Disaster Reduction and Recovery
GFSI	Global Food Security Index
GHI	Global Hunger Index

GNI	Gross National Income
GRFC	Global Report on Food Crises
GYD	Guyana Dollars
HDI	Human Development Index
HFLACI	Hunger-Free Latin America and the Caribbean Initiative
HRI	Hotel Restaurants and Institutional
ICT	Information and Communication Technologies
IDB	Inter-American Development Bank
IEA	International Energy Agency
IFAD	International Fund for Agricultural Development
IICA	Inter-American Institute for Cooperation on Agriculture
IMF	International Monetary Fund
LCDS	Low Carbon Development Strategy
OECS	Organisation of Eastern Caribbean States
PoU	Prevalence of Undernourishment
PPP	Purchasing Power Parity or Private Public Partnership
RATC	Regional Agro-Tech Campus
RSDS	Regional Strategy for the Development of Statistics
SDG/SDGs	Sustainable Development Goals
SIDS	Small Island Developing States
SMEs	Small and Medium-Sized Enterprises
SOFI	State of Food Security and Nutrition
SPS	Sanitary and Phytosanitary
STI	Science, Technology and Innovation
SWM	Sustainable Wildlife Management
USAID	United States Agency for International Development
USD	United States Dollars
VAT	Value Added Tax
WEF	World Economic Forum
WFP	World Food Programme

About the Author

Dr. Mohamed Irfaan Ali is the current President of the Co-operative Republic of Guyana. He is the holder of the B.A. (Hons.) in Business and Management from University of Sunderland (U.K.); a Post-Graduate Certificate in Finance from Anglia Ruskin University (U.K.); LL.M in Commercial Law from University of Salford (U.K.); M.A. in Human Resource Planning from GGS Indraprastha University (New Delhi, India); and a Ph.D in Urban Planning from University of the West Indies (Trinidad & Tobago). Dr. Ali also holds an honorary doctorate from GGS Indraprastha University (New Delhi, India).

President Ali served as the Chair of Caribbean Community (CARICOM) Conference of Heads of Government (2024). On February 13, 2024, he chaired the UN Security Council 9547th meeting of the Council on Threats to International Peace and Security.

Dr. Ali is the first recipient of the Inter-American Institute for Cooperation on Agriculture (IICA) Award. In 2023, Dr. Ali was conferred with the Pravasi Bharatiya Samman by the Government of India. In the same year, the Government of Barbados conferred on him the Order of Freedom of Barbados. He is also the recipient of the Legacy Award from the American Foundation for the University of the West Indies (AFUW); the International Leadership Award for deepening democracy from the International Forum on African and Caribbean Leadership; and the Caribbean Global Leader Award (2024) in the People's Choice category.

Author's Note

Food security remains of vital importance to the people of the Caribbean. However, consisting of a constellation of Small-Island Developing and Low-lying Coastal States, the Caribbean Community remains vulnerable to climate, economic, energy, and food shocks, the latter of which is mainly on account of the region's extreme dependence on extra-regional food imports.

Regional food security has long been on the agenda of the Caribbean Community. In recognition of the ever-increasing regional food imports bill and the deleterious effects of the COVID-19 coronavirus pandemic on regional food systems and food security, Guyana tabled a paper during the 32nd Inter-Sessional Meeting of the Conference of Heads of Government of the Caribbean Community, which was held virtually, in February 2021. Entitled, "Advancing the Caribbean Agri-Food Systems Agenda: Prioritizing Regional Food and Nutrition Security," the paper examined and made proposals to address the challenges relating to Caribbean food security.

The Conference endorsed the development of an agri-food system strategy involving a "strategic partnership with regional private sector bodies to promote commercialisation of the sector and supported the implementation of policy recommendations in that regard." It also mandated the establishment of a Special Ministerial Task Force on Food Production and Food Security (MTF).

The MTF, in turn, has helped to propel the goal established by CARICOM Heads of Government of reducing the region's food import bill by 25% by 2025. This book has benefitted from and builds upon the ongoing work of the MTF and the outcomes of Agri-Investment Conferences hosted within the region.

This book was developed against the backdrop of increasing global food insecurity and hunger, both of which have been exacerbated by the combined and interlinked effects of the COVID-19 pandemic, global conflicts, disruptions to global supply chains, climate change, and surging energy prices.

The Caribbean has not been spared from the effects of these developments. Indeed, the spate of global crises has weakened food systems and undermined regional food security.

The book dissects the state of regional food security by analyzing the challenges posed by the region's high dependence on imported food, its food security vulnerabilities, the need for increased private investment in agriculture, and the sector's susceptibility to climate change.

In examining the state of regional food security, the book provides country briefs addressing the food security situation of every member state, as well as relevant economic indicators and concise overviews of production and investment in each country's agricultural sector. The country briefs also examine the impact of climate change on each country's food production.

The end product of this book is the compilation of pertinent policy recommendations to guide the region's priority actions in advancing food security, as well as an adumbration of ongoing initiatives.

None of the recommendations is contentious; they include investing in research and development, forging partnerships, commercialising food supply, dismantling technical barriers to the trade in agricultural products, de-risking the agricultural sector, and improving transportation and logistics. Most of these have previously engaged the attention of the community.

Time, unfortunately, is not on our side. Urgent action is needed to boost regional food and nutrition security. The onus is on the leadership of our community to take decisions and to drive actions that would better insulate the region from exogenous food shocks, reduce its dependence on extra-regional food imports, and strengthen food and nutrition security.

Mohamed Irfaan Ali
President of the Co-operative Republic of Guyana

Message I

The world is off track in achieving the sustainable development goals (SDGs). Resilient and sustainable agriculture and access to healthy diets are essential to eradicate hunger and poverty. In recent years, a series of successive crises have hit the world, negatively affecting Latin America and the Caribbean agri-food systems and beyond.

Up to 828 million people suffered hunger globally in 2021 — 150 million more than in 2019. In Latin America and the Caribbean, 56.5 million people suffered from hunger in 2021. This is an increase of 13.2 million people from 2019 and 20.6 million from 2015 when countries collectively agreed to eradicate hunger by 2030 as one of the SDG targets.

In this context, it is worrying that in 2021 Latin America and the Caribbean had a higher prevalence of moderate or severe food insecurity than the global rate, as well as a higher cost of a healthy diet compared to the world average.

This book shows how the recent global crises have impacted agri-food systems and food insecurity worldwide, particularly in Caribbean countries. It presents statistics and current trends considering food production, imports, investments in agriculture, and the impacts of the climate crisis on agri-food systems.

The book also presents the main food security and nutrition challenges facing the region, including the effects of the COVID-19 pandemic on the economy and supply chains, slow GDP growth in countries, income inequality, and high food inflation. In addition, it analyses the evolving impacts of the war in Ukraine, which has exacerbated the increase in food prices, affecting food import-dependent countries more, particularly in the Caribbean, and has also led to an increase in fertiliser and energy prices. Although the drop in international food, energy and fertilizer prices in recent months has provided some relief for countries, prices are still above 2021 levels.

Improving food security requires urgent action by different sectors of the agri-food system. Countries should consider the most cost-effective and efficient solutions, considering the national context and the limited resources available. Producer-oriented agri-food markets and trade, as well as consumer-oriented policies, can contribute to addressing this challenge.

This book contains recommendations for developing agriculture, technologies, and innovation for sustainable production. It highlights the importance of incorporating the private sector and small-scale producers through investment, financing, and capacity-building systems. Finally, it offers recommendations to advance food transport and logistics, facilitating physical and economic access to food, especially healthy diets.

Finally, this work highlights the food insecurity situation in the world, with a particular focus on the Caribbean, and provides concrete recommendations to improve food security and nutrition. The Food and Agriculture Organization (FAO) of the United Nations is firmly committed to supporting members in the design and implementation of public policies to transform agri-food systems to make them more efficient, inclusive, resilient and sustainable and to leave no one behind. To achieve these objectives, we must ensure better production, better nutrition, a better environment and a better life for all. We need to act now through science and innovation and transformative investments in global agri-food systems. The millions of people suffering from hunger and malnutrition cannot wait.

Qu Dongyu
Director-General,
Food and Agriculture Organization (FAO)

Message II

The world is going backwards in its efforts to eradicate poverty and hunger. As shown in the Regional Overview Food Security and Nutrition in Latin America and the Caribbean 2022 (FAO, 2022), the prevalence of undernourishment is increasing and is now higher than in 2015 when countries first agreed to eradicate hunger by 2030 as one of the SDG targets. In the Caribbean, between 2014 and 2021, hunger increased by 2.3 percentage points, affecting 16.4% of its population by 2021.

The Panorama 2022 concluded that moderate or severe food insecurity in the world has increased consistently since 2014. In Latin America and the Caribbean, it is rising more rapidly than in the rest of the world. Moreover, compared to the world's average, moderate or severe food insecurity in the region exceeded the world's average by 11.3 percentage points in 2021. While in 2021, the gap between men and women was higher, the prevalence of moderate or severe food insecurity in the Caribbean (64%) was higher than the region and more than twice the world average, influenced by Haitian levels.

Nevertheless, the Caribbean has also made progress in nutritional indicators. The prevalence of stunting in children under five years of age decreased between 2000 and 2020, and the prevalence of overweight in children under five years of age, although increased, was below the regional average in 2020. However, obesity in adults reached a proportion similar to the regional level, which is higher compared to the world average.

Latin America and the Caribbean not only register high levels of inequality but also record the highest cost of a healthy diet. The average cost of a healthy diet in the region is estimated at US$3.89 per person per day according to the last estimation in the Panorama 2022, which is the highest compared to world averages. In the Caribbean, the cost of a healthy diet is estimated at US$4.23, and it increased by 4.1% between 2019 and 2020.

The increase in poverty as a consequence of the COVID-19 pandemic, slow GDP growth, high-income inequality, and high food inflation is making healthy diets even less affordable. In addition, the increase in prices for food and fertilisers was exacerbated because the war in Ukraine has affected the region, especially the more food import-dependent countries.

Due to this complexity, no single policy can provide the solution independently. Therefore, what is needed is a combination of international cooperation, regional integration, and multisectoral actions involving all stakeholders of the agri-food system.

The 7th Summit of Heads of State and Government of the Community of Latin American and Caribbean States (CELAC) concluded with a declaration from 33 member states, which reinforces a regional commitment to guarantee food security, supporting agricultural and rural development, promoting the increase of sustainable food production and the availability of food, as well as a fairer, more transparent, equitable and predictable international trade system.

In 2015, the 33 CELAC countries approved the Food Security and Nutrition Plan, and now, we put FAO's support again at the government's disposal to analyse other partners' progress and update it for the current context, and extend it to reach the 2030 targets, as it was agreed in the Buenos Aires Declaration.

It is noteworthy that the Caribbean Community (CARICOM) is implementing the agri-food systems strategy in member states to help achieve a reduction of the Caribbean's large food import bill by 25% by 2025. In this regard, FAO is supporting the development of priority value chains to contribute to reducing the region's food import bill. It is doing so by working with governments and key stakeholders in designing and upgrading strategies as well as good practices and opportunities for attracting investment to help boost intra-regional trade.

This book provides an in-depth analysis of food security in the Caribbean and includes policy recommendations for moving forward towards this target. Strengthening the technologies, innovation, and investments for sustainable food production and the availability of nutritious foods will contribute to CARICOM's food security goal.

In a global context of adverse humanitarian conditions, Latin America and the Caribbean Region face important challenges in eradicating hunger and malnutrition in all its forms. Despite progress in the region to reduce child undernutrition in the past decades, hunger and food insecurity need urgent regional cooperation and agri-food system transformation to improve the affordability of healthy diets and fight against climate change.

Mario Lubetkin
Director General — Latin America and the Caribbean,
Food and Agriculture Organization (FAO)

Preface

Introduction: A Vital Blueprint for Food and Human Security in the 21st Century

Amitav Acharya

*Distinguished Professor of International Relations and
the UNESCO Chair in Transnational Challenges and Governance
American University
Washington, DC*

This book, written by the President of Guyana, H.E. Dr Mohamed Irfaan Ali, makes a new, timely and major contribution to the understanding of, and response to, one of the most critical challenges facing the current world order: how to achieve freedom from hunger through food security.

While the subject is not new, there cannot be a more opportune moment to revisit this topic. In the past few years, the world has seen a 'return of geopolitics', especially with the Russia–Ukraine War, the Israel–Hamas conflict and the growing rivalry between the US and China, the world's two most powerful nations. Adding to this is the challenge of climate change and pandemics, as vividly illustrated by the COVID-19 outbreak.

However, while the nations of the Global North remain preoccupied with their national and international security issues, the concerns of the Global South remain centred on human security.

While national and international security prioritises the security of states, human security stresses the security of people. The idea of human security has two main aspects: 'freedom from fear' and 'freedom from want'. The two are interrelated. But, for developing countries, as I had pointed out in a speech to the UN General Assembly,[1] 'freedom from want' is more people-centred since hunger and underdevelopment directly affect common people rather than elites and make society more prone to conflict and violence. And few things are more important to 'freedom from want' than the elimination of hunger through universal and unconditional food security.

To elaborate, the idea of human security was first put forward three decades ago in the UNDP's 1994 Human Development Report. This report outlined seven core elements of human security: (1) Economic security; (2) Food security; (3) Health security; (4) Environmental security; (5) Personal security; (6) Community security; and (7) Political security.

In the UNDP report, food security was defined as a condition where "all people at all times have both physical and economic access to basic food. This requires not just enough food to go round. It requires that people have ready access to food-that they have an "entitlement" to food, by growing it for themselves, by buying it or by taking advantage of a public food distribution system. The availability of food is thus a necessary condition of security-but not a sufficient one. People can still starve even when enough food is available-as has happened during many famines."

This definition echoes the Food and Agriculture Organization (FAO), which, as mentioned in this book, defines food security as a *"situation which exists when all people, at all times, have physical, social and*

---

[1] Text of Speech by Professor Amitav Acharya, UNESCO Chair in Transnational Challenges and Governance, America University, at the "Informal Thematic Debate of the 65th Session of the United Nations General Assembly on Human Security", New York, 14 April 2011, https://www.un.org/en/ga/president/65/pdf/calendar/20110414-humansec.pdf.

economic access to sufficient, safe, and nutritious food that meets their dietary needs and food preferences for an active and healthy life."

The emphasis on food security is further reflected in the Sustainable Development Goals (SDGs). Goal number 2 of the SDGs is to "End hunger, achieve food security and improved nutrition and promote sustainable agriculture."

Despite such recognition of the importance of food security, it remains an unfulfilled goal. Food insecurity remains a special challenge to the nations of the Global South, including small states like those of the Caribbean. As President Ali starkly reminds us in this book, food insecurity in severe or moderate forms affects nearly a quarter of the 17 million people of the Caribbean, and "eradicating or attenuating the burden of food insecurity in the Region is far from attainable."

Developments in the past few years have shown the acute vulnerability of the nations of the Global South to food supply disruptions. The war in Ukraine has affected Global South nations in a hugely disproportionate manner, especially by cutting off supplies of agricultural exports from Ukraine, one of the world's major food suppliers. This is a reminder that small nations remain especially vulnerable to distant conflicts and need to build up their self-reliance and resilience against such disruptions.

The Israel–Hamas conflict is another reminder of the world's unfulfilled quest for food security. Due to massive and relentless Israeli strikes and Israel's decision to cut off or severely limit food supplies to Gaza, Gaza is suffering from famine. This is a reminder that despite all the advances in transportation and connectivity, the delivery of food in conflict zones remains a challenge.

Therefore, national action and regional cooperation are vital to the security and well-being of Global South nations, including Caribbean states. Unlike the EU, the nations of the Global South are less worried about free trade than about ensuring the basic necessities of life, including food.

The old world order led by the Western nations, which has been called the 'US-led Liberal International Order', is going through profound changes. The relative power and influence of the Western nations are declining while those of leading non-Western nations, such as China and India, and other BRICS nations are rising. But these changes have not eliminated the insecurity of the world's smaller and weaker nations. If anything, it has made them more vulnerable to global shocks and power transitions. The gap between the world's richer and poorer nations is widening, and even within the Global South, there is a widening gulf between the 'Power South', such as many of the BRICS nations, and the 'poor South', which includes the Least Developed Countries (LDCs).

At the same time, we are entering into a Multiplex World, a world without a hegemonic power or bloc. This is a world of diversity and connectivity led by multiple actors, not only great powers but also small states and regional groupings, which have a role to play in ensuring their own regional peace and stability and thereby contributing to the global order. With major war returning to the heart of Europe, the security and well-being of smaller states cannot depend on the goodwill of and handouts from the wealthier nations of the Global North, especially when they are ever more concerned about their own national security challenges. Indeed, the return of geopolitics may detract from the realisation of human security goals. Hence, the smaller states of the world have to step up their own action, through national, bilateral and multilateral measures, to ensure their survival and well-being in the face of global shocks and challenges, such as climate change, pandemics and Great Power rivalry.

It is in this context that this book by President Ali is of critical significance. It offers a vital blueprint for economic progress, sustainable development and human security for the Caribbean region with implications for the entire world. It not only identifies multiple dimensions of food insecurity in the Caribbean but also suggests practical steps to alleviate if not eliminate this scourge. The book's policy recommendations, such as establishing a regional food hub, removing technical barriers to agricultural and food supply, strengthening regional connectivity to smoothen the flow of food items and creating an Agricultural Catastrophe Fund, are essential steps to ensure food security and guard against future shocks. These recommendations are relevant not only to the Caribbean region but also to other parts of the Global South, such as Africa, where food security remains a challenge.

In sum, global food security and Caribbean food security remain an unmet challenge in the 21st century. The concept of human security offers an important framework for analysing, addressing and responding to this challenge. Without food security, there can be no human security, and without human security, there can be no global security and world order. Any claim that humankind has made progress towards freedom and welfare becomes less meaningful when one looks at the lack of food security in the world today. This is why this book offers a powerful and timely impetus to advancing the agenda of food security, the realisation of the SDGs, and the fulfilment of the concept of human security in the 21st century.

Chapter 1

Introduction

"War is tipping a fragile world towards mass hunger. Fixing that is everyone's business."

— *The Economist* (2022)

Global hunger might have been at its highest level in 2022 due to the onset of several global problems. Specifically, the war in Ukraine coupled with the COVID-19 pandemic and the increase in climate-related events have exposed the fragility of the global supply chain and its food system. High food prices coupled with displaced labour, soaring energy, and fertilizer costs have added upward pressure on cost of living and food insecurity, especially among developing countries.

These occurrences seem to unravel most of the gains in the battle against hunger. Over the past decade, the number of persons living in hunger has declined by more than 100 million (*The Economist*, 2022). In contrast, from 2020 to 2022, acute food insecurity in 79 countries alone increased from 278 million to a record 349 million people. Compared to the pre-COVID-19 pandemic levels in 2019, the increase in 2022 represents an addition of almost 200 million people. Overall, more than 900,000 people globally are battling famine-like conditions. This indicates a 10-fold increase in these cases compared to five years ago, begging the need for an immediate response and solution (WFP, 2022). Even more worrisome is that international organisations known to help fight hunger, such as the World Food Programme, are now faced with multiple new challenges. For instance, aid is unlikely to meet a large number of people living with acute hunger due to the current logistical supply chain crisis. Furthermore, the sharp increase in inflation coupled with higher energy costs is also likely to ebb away the levels of available funding set aside to help fight global hunger.

The causes of the current food crisis represent a combination of several factors. One is the conflict in Ukraine, where almost 60% of the world's hungry population lives in war-affected zones. The war has proven devastating to the livelihood of these people through labour displacement and wrecked economies. Other factors include the rise in climate-related events and higher fertiliser prices, which are currently at a 10-year high.

The global food security crisis has not spared the Caribbean Region. To a large extent, the region is considered vulnerable to climate change and global shocks due to its geographical location and dependence on imports. Food prices in the region have been on the increase due to a combination of several factors ranging from the increase in pests and plant-related diseases to a surge in climate-related events and inflation coupled with higher share levels of food imports (from 20.1% in 2019 to 24.8% in 2022). Notably, there has also been an overall decline in private sector investment in agriculture (as a share of total domestic credit), moving from 2.3% in 2005 to 1.3% in 2020.

This book presents a series of policy recommendations to help address the current food security crisis in the Caribbean Region. For the purpose of analysis, which takes the form of observing several explanatory food security-related variables, data are sourced mainly from the World Bank, FAOSTAT, and IMF, ranging from 2005 to 2021.

The book is organised as follows: Chapter 2 provides an overview of the global food security crisis, focusing on some lead causes. Chapter 3 takes the analysis to the regional level, providing a brief macroeconomic overview while examining the state of food security. Chapter 4 looks at the analysis from a country-level perspective. Chapter 5 outlines a series of policy recommendations for the current food crisis. Finally, Chapter 6 highlights some of the works already in the pipeline and the way forward.

Chapter 2

The Global Picture: Food Security — Challenges and Limitations

The current global food crisis remains a major concern for many countries, especially those in the developing world (von Grebmer *et al.*, 2022). The Food and Agriculture Organization (FAO) defines food security as a "situation which exists when all people, at all times, have physical, social and economic access to sufficient, safe, and nutritious food that meets their dietary needs and food preferences for an active and healthy life" (FAO, 2009). Usually, there are four pillars of food security: availability, utilisation, access, and stability (Jennifer Clapp *et al.*, 2022).

Globally, food, agriculture, land, and ocean systems account for $10 trillion or over 12% of GDP and 40% of all jobs (World Economic Forum, 2022). According to the 2022 Global Hunger Index (GHI) report,[1] there has been a slowdown in reducing global hunger during the last three years. In fact, it is perceived that overall progress has stagnated and, in some countries, deteriorated. For instance, in Somalia, two districts are at risk of famine due to years of conflict, prolonged drought, and population displacement. Compounding this predicament is the likelihood of a

---

[1] The GHI measures and tracks hunger at the global, regional, and national levels. A score of 50 and above is considered extremely alarming: 35–49.9 alarming, 20–34.9 serious, 10–19.9 moderate, and less than 9.9 low. The scores of the index are based on four components: undernourishment, child stunting, child wasting, and child mortality. The higher the GHI score, the higher the severity of hunger.

decline in humanitarian assistance to the country. If immediate actions are not taken, significant amounts of deaths could occur.

In another report, the Global Report on Food Crises 2022 Mid-Year Update indicated that the number of people requiring urgent humanitarian assistance is expected to increase to 205.1 million in 45 of the 53 surveyed countries (GRFC, 2022). Compared to 2019, in 2020, almost 46 million more people in Africa and 14 million more in Latin America and the Caribbean have been affected by hunger, nearly doubling the number of people exposed to severe food insecurity compared to 2014 (FAO, 2022).

Particularly as it relates to the prevalence of undernourishment (PoU), as of 2021, almost 828 million people lacked access to sufficient calories. Notably, from 2019 to 2020, PoU increased from 8.4% to 9.9%, respectively (FAO, 2022), and is likely to increase further, given the current global conditions. These crises have manifested at a time when a large share of the developing world is still reeling from underlying and fundamental challenges such as widespread poverty, inequality in infrastructure, low agricultural productivity, reduced fiscal space, supply chain volatility, and even chronic hunger (von Grebmer *et al.*, 2022).

In line with these findings, the Global Food Security Index (GFSI)[2] reflected a decline of 4% in the affordability pillar from 2019 to 2020 due to a sharp rise in food costs, declining trade freedom, and decreased funding for food safety nets (Global Food Security Index, 2022). Based on the latest forecast, the global food security scenario is expected to remain bleak, with almost 660 million people facing hunger in 2030 (FAO, 2022).

2.1. Inflation

Globally, food prices have been on the increase over the past few years, especially among low- and middle-income countries. Specifically, around 84.2% of low-income countries recorded a sharp increase in food prices between July and October 2022 of almost 5%. This phenomenon was also present in about 93% of lower-middle-income countries and 93% of upper-middle-income countries, with many of these countries recording

---

[2] The GFSI evaluates food security in 113 countries based on affordability, availability, quality and safety, and sustainability and adaptation.

double-digit inflation. Notably, advanced economies did not escape the predicament, with about 85.5% experiencing high levels of food price inflation (World Bank, 2022). Higher food prices have driven millions into extreme poverty, further stoking hunger and malnutrition. According to the IMF CPI database, food and energy prices have been the primary drivers behind the surge in global inflation to almost 10% in 2022 (WEF, 2022a).

According to a survey by McKinsey (2022b), inflation and global conflicts are two major threats to economic growth and development over the next 12 months. For instance, in Europe, energy volatility in tandem with inflation is considered the most significant threat to higher food prices. In the future, global food prices are expected to increase further due to higher inflation, tightening financial conditions, the war in Ukraine, and the COVID-19 pandemic.

2.2. War in Ukraine

Geopolitical and climate-related events have affected the resilience of the world's food system. The war in Ukraine (a country situated in one of the world's foremost breadbasket regions) is seen as a major threat to global food security primarily because of its proximity to the Black Sea, a central trans-shipment hub for wheat and fertilizer. While indeed a deal was reached in July 2022 to free approximately 20 million tonnes of grains stuck in the Black Sea ports, major concerns remain around the inland bottleneck of the region, which is likely to affect logistics and the supply of grains to customers.

Globally, because of the war and the lacklustre performance of some of the other major agricultural-producing countries (Russia and Brazil, for example), a deficit in the global supply of grain exports of up to 40 million metric tonnes is projected in 2023 (McKinsey, 2022b). This concern is further compounded by a decline in fertiliser supply, particularly from Russia and Belarus, which poses a possible threat to yield output and production (Behnassi and El Haiba, 2022).

Higher energy costs are also expected to exert upward pressure on food prices, potentially pushing millions into acute food insecurity (Behnassi and El Haiba, 2022). Notably, Russia and Ukraine account for almost 25% of global wheat exports, 15% of corn exports, and 75% of sunflower oil (OECD, 2022). This, of course, could engender and, in some cases, exacerbate trade-related problems. For a start, countries with low food supplies may become reluctant to export. Furthermore, international donor agencies may find it even more challenging to distribute sufficient food aid due to higher prices, spelling disaster, especially for those countries that are greatly exposed to famine (Behnassi and El Haiba, 2022).

2.3. COVID-19 Pandemic

The past 18 months have brought about unprecedented global challenges with the advent of the COVID-19 virus. This pandemic engendered a global health crisis, weakened the global food system, and unravelled years of achievements under the sustainable development goals (SDGs) (FAO, 2022a).

In 2020, the prevalence of food insecurity was equal to the combined amount for the preceding five years or an increase of about 320 million people in just one year. A staggering 21% of Africa was faced with hunger. The pandemic also worsened inequality and the food insecurity gender gap, with food insecurity among women being 10% higher than among men in 2020 (FAO, 2022a).

According to the 2021 State of Food Security and Nutrition (SOFI), the effect of COVID-19 on food security is palpable and detrimental. Given the existing challenges before the pandemic, achieving the UN 2030 Agenda of eliminating hunger is poised to become more complicated, threatening millions of people's food security and nutrition worldwide (FAO, 2022).

The COVID-19 pandemic has tested the fiscal limits of many countries, especially the developing world. Among the poorest households, where almost 70% of revenue is spent on food, the pandemic has weakened access to food security, affecting children's cognitive development. For instance, a recent survey in Ethiopia shows that almost 80% of households did not have enough savings to meet their food needs (Laborde *et al.*, 2020).

2.4. Climate Change

The effect of climate change on global food production is well documented. In fact, increasing global temperature is expected to expose the world to further climate hazards and food insecurity, leading to higher poverty levels, especially in vulnerable regions (Portner *et al.*, 2022). Among low-income countries, the threat is even greater for those that are susceptible to higher temperatures and lack of fresh water (Kogo *et al.*, 2021).

In a world with a 2°C increase in surface temperature, the negative effect of climate change on food production will be even greater, especially on the terrestrial food production system. Under this scenario, crop cultivation and livestock areas will likely become unsuitable. This is due to the fact that higher CO_2 tends to reduce essential soil nutrition, affecting the yield of some crops. The negative effect could be extended to include aquatic food services.

Other dimensions of the effects of climate change on food security include higher prices, lower food diversity, and reduced agricultural production. Regions with the highest risks include Africa, small island states such as the Caribbean, and South Asia.

2.5. Logistics and Supply Chain Crisis

The outbreak of COVID-19 has led to the disruption of the global supply chain, leading to food shortages and delays in the delivery of goods (Tietze *et al.*, 2022). The build-up of vessels along maritime ports, high freight rates, and higher fuel prices have been some of the principal drivers behind the supply chain crisis. Another factor is the changes in household expenditure patterns, leading to the growth in e-commerce. In the U.S., almost 85% of household stimulus payments were spent on e-commerce goods due to the travelling restrictions and quarantine. Globally, this created geographical shifts in supply and demand (WEF, 2022b). In 2020, e-commerce sales as a percentage of retail sales were almost 32%, a 15% increase relative to 2019.

The supply chain crisis is further compounded by the lack of labour, truck drivers, and even warehousing (Kent and Haralambides, 2022). Based on a recent McKinsey survey (2022b), supply chain turmoil has been identified as one of the greatest threats to the growth of companies and countries' economies, even greater than the pandemic, war, and labour shortage.

2.6. The Global Energy Crisis

Energy markets are tightening because of the rapid rebound of the global economy following the post-pandemic opening-up of economies. The surge in energy demand, coupled with low supply levels, had led to a global energy crisis. Other factors, such as Russia's invasion of Ukraine, climate change, and the decision by oil and gas companies and some of the major oil-exporting countries to scale back on investment in the industry, appeared to have exacerbated the crisis. Specifically, the price of natural gas soared to record heights, with oil reaching its highest levels since 2008. The spillover effects have led to higher inflation, poverty, and even constrained economic growth to the point where some countries are now on the brink of recession.

While today's energy crisis shares many similarities to the 1970s, one of the key differences is that the present crisis involves all fossil fuels, unlike the 1970s, which was primarily concerned with oil. Secondly, the current global economy is much more interlinked, which has intensified the impact of the shock. Due to these conditions, this may be the world's first global energy crisis.

Energy is used in the agriculture and food industries for various purposes, from electricity for water irrigation systems to fuel for food processing equipment, transportation, and distribution. Even the application of pesticides and fertilizers requires a large amount of energy. Therefore, because of higher energy costs and fertilizer prices, the cost of food production and, ultimately, food prices will inevitably increase (IEA, 2022).

Notably, the world was already finding it difficult to provide an equitable energy supply to all prior to the energy crisis. Almost 770 million people lacked access to electricity, which is a major deterrent to achieving established development goals and reducing poverty. Furthermore, around 2.4 billion people across the globe still cook using open fires or inefficient stoves fuelled by kerosene, coal, or biomass (WHO, 2022). Indeed, this could lead to adverse health consequences, affecting the most vulnerable groups in society (WFP, 2022a).

Chapter 3

The Regional Picture

3.1. Food Imports

This section examines the food security environment within the Caribbean Region from an economic perspective. The Caribbean[1] Community is home to almost 17 million people, out of whom around 4.1 million are moderately or severely food insecure (CARICOM Today, 2022). Notably, the region remains susceptible to outmigration, international debt, climate change, and high imports (FAO, 2022b). So far, eradicating or attenuating the burden of food insecurity in the region is far from attainable, though several initiatives and action plans have been endorsed (Mohammadi et al., 2022), such as The World Food Summit in 1996, Millennium Development Goals in 2000, Hunger-Free Latin America and the Caribbean Initiative (HFLACI) in 2005, and Regional Food and Nutrition Security Policy (RFNSP) in 2010 (Mohammadi et al., 2022, p. 3).

In the Caribbean, extreme weather events have negatively affected food production, prompting the need for more progressive policies and regulations. Specifically, these events have caused significant losses in agricultural production, causing many countries in the region to rely heavily on food imports and financial aid (Ganpat, 2014). As shown in Figure 3.1, around half of the region's states have cultivated only 50% of their land available for agriculture.

---

[1] The Caribbean region in this book comprises Antigua and Barbuda, Aruba, The Bahamas, Barbados, Belize, Dominica, Grenada, Guyana, Haiti, Jamaica, Saint Kitts and Nevis, Saint Lucia, Saint Vincent and the Grenadines, Suriname, and Trinidad and Tobago.

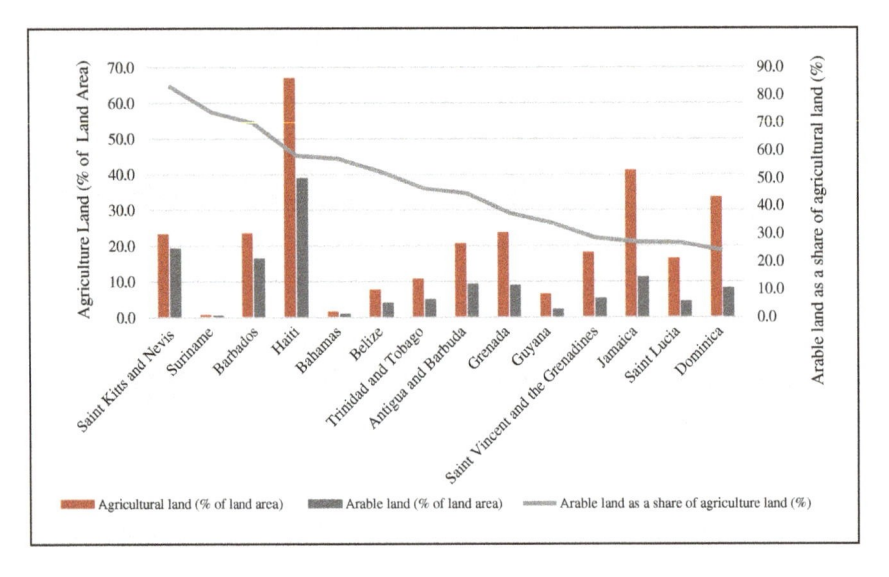

Figure 3.1. Agricultural and arable land of various CARICOM member states (2020).

Note: The left axis of the graph captures agricultural land (% of land area) and arable land (% of land area), respectively. The right axis shows arable land as a share of agricultural land. All data points are as of 2020.
Source: World Bank Data.

Among the region's major factors affecting food security are lower land productivity, inclement weather patterns, high-energy costs, and lack of international competitiveness (Beckford, 2012). The latter has contributed to lower revenue, negatively affecting the region's ability to reach its import demand. This is particularly worrisome since the region relies heavily on food imports.

As shown in Figure 3.2, on average, the Caribbean Region increased its dependency on food imports in 2020 relative to 2019 before reaching 25% in 2021, the highest level in over a decade. The increase in 2020 corresponds to the arrival of the COVID-19 pandemic, energy crisis, and supply chain crisis. According to the International Trade Centre, the

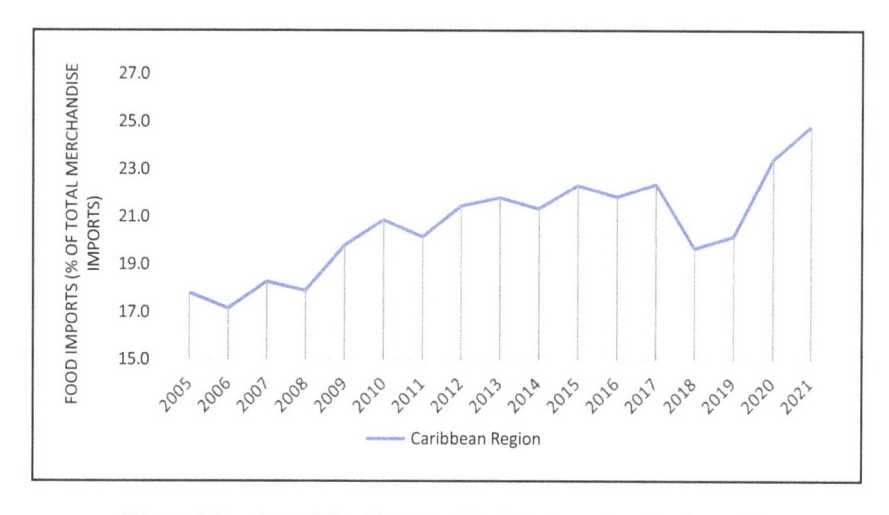

Figure 3.2. Annual food imports (% of total merchandise imports).

Note: The blue line represents the average food imports (% of total merchandise imports) for the Caribbean Region.
Source: World Bank Data.

region's total merchandise imports in 2021 amounted to around US$35 billion, the second-highest recorded level since 2002. Of this amount, food imports represent US$4.9 billion, an increase of US$600 million compared to 2020. The increased reliance on food imports is a testament to the region's inability to satisfy its domestic food consumption demand, a key challenge to achieving food security (CARICOM, 2020). Critically, the increased dependence on food imports exposes the region to negative externalities such as high prices.

As is evident in Figure 3.3, in 2020, Haiti exhibited the largest share of food imports as a percentage of total merchandise imports, followed by Saint Lucia. However, in 2021, the share of food imports for Saint Lucia increased by almost 40 percentage points and eclipsed that of Haiti. Conversely, Guyana is seen as having the lowest share of food imports in both 2020 and 2021.

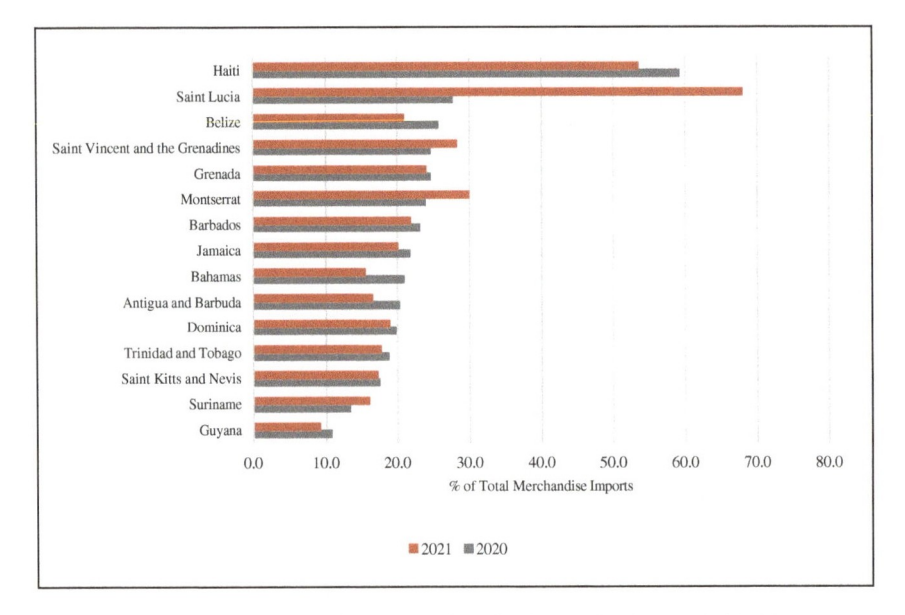

Figure 3.3. Food imports (% of total merchandise imports) of selected Caribbean countries for 2020 and 2021.

Source: World Bank Data.

3.2. Macroeconomic Overview

The global outlook appears volatile, with many countries still reeling from the COVID-19 pandemic. Additionally, climate change has strengthened its grip on many parts of the world, decimating agricultural production while increasing the risk of food insecurity. The war in Ukraine has further contributed to global volatility by unleashing adverse effects on food prices and energy costs.

It has been suggested that countries must undertake monetary policy-tightening endeavours to regain some sense of normalcy and stability. However, while this may be the case, for most Caribbean countries, this could result in tighter fiscal space, exacerbating the present economic burden that has plagued the region.

The present macroeconomic environment of the region is expected to be further tested by the surge in food prices, which has triggered higher import bills, larger trade deficits, and higher levels of inequality and poverty. For instance, 45% of Haiti's population is faced with food crises or emergencies (World Bank, 2022b). Some of the major drivers of low food

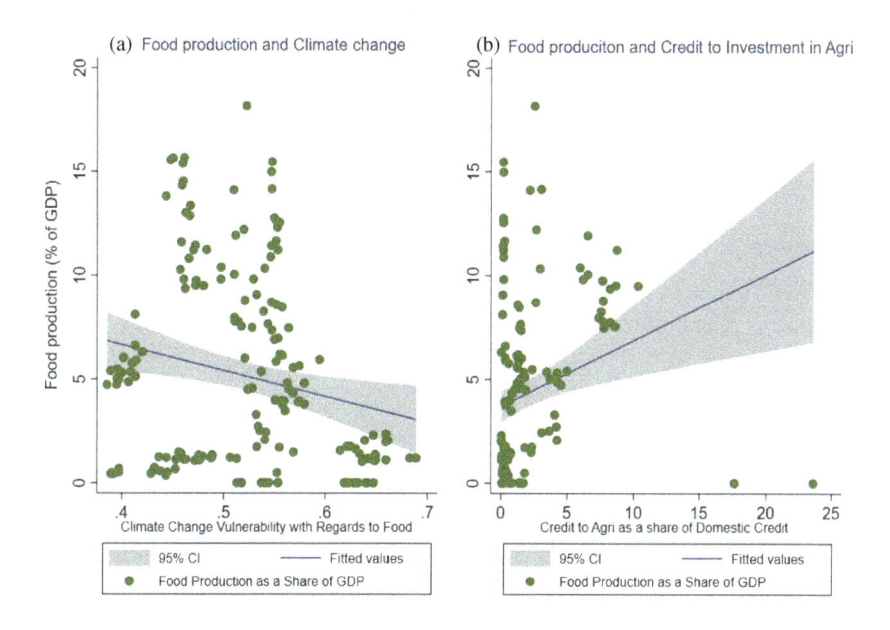

Figure 3.4. Food security vulnerability and share of investment in agriculture, respectively, on the share of food production in the Caribbean Region from 2005 to 2021.

Note: (a) shows the effect of food security vulnerability (to climate change) on the share of food production. The straight line represents the fitted line with a 95% confidence interval. Similarly, (b) shows the effect of increased credit to the agriculture sector (as a share of total domestic credit) on the share of food production. Data on the value of food production (in USD current price) as a share of GDP is sourced from FAOSTAT and World Bank, respectively. An increase in this indicator represents an increase in food production. Data on climate change vulnerability with regard to food security (or climate change vulnerability with regard to food)[2] is sourced from the ND-Gain Dataset by the University of Notre Dame. An increase in the score signifies an increase in food security vulnerability to climate-related events. Finally, data on credit to agriculture as a share of domestic credit is sourced from the FAOSTAT. An increase in this variable represents an increase in lending by commercial banks to the private sector for investment in agriculture.
Source: Author's calculation using data from FAOSTAT, World Bank Data and the ND-Gain Dataset.

production include the increased vulnerability of food security to climate change and a lower share of credit to the agriculture sector for private investments. As shown in Figure 3.4, the increase in food security vulnerability to climate change seems to negatively affect food production in the Caribbean, as in the case of a lower share of credit to the agriculture

---

[2] This indicator is used interchangeably with "Food Security Vulnerability to Climate Change Impacts".

sector. Even though the observed relationship between the share of food production and the other two variables is not robust, the patterns are largely consistent with the literature.

3.2.1. *Private sector investment in agriculture*

Private sector investment in agriculture is crucial if the Caribbean's agriculture sector is to achieve its 2025 goal of reducing food imports by 25% while increasing output by another US$1.5 billion (CARICOM Today, 2022a). Based on preliminary assessments, reducing the region's food import bill by 25% in 2025 would require a total private sector investment of around US$7.5 billion.

As shown in Figure 3.5, during the period from 2005 to 2018, the region saw a steady decline in the share of domestic credit attributable to agriculture from about 6% at the beginning of the period to less than 2% at the end. While the share has since rebounded to slightly above 3% in

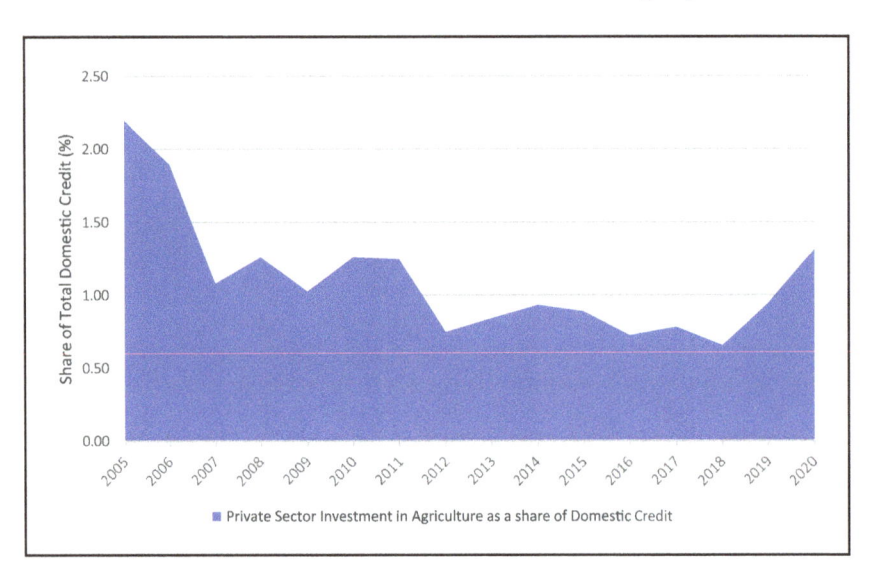

Figure 3.5. Average credit to agriculture (as a share of domestic credit) from 2005 to 2020 for the region.

Note: Private sector investment in agriculture as a share of domestic credit is used interchangeably with credit to agriculture as a share of domestic credit.
Source: FAOSTAT.

2020, it represents about half of the 2005 level. Indeed, this decline is worrisome and suggests that the Caribbean's 2025 target of reducing its food import bill by 25% may be at risk if urgent actions are not taken to boost private sector investment in agriculture.

3.2.2. *Inflation and public debt*

The region's economy is expected to face added pressure due to increased global inflation. Figure 3.6 shows that the regional level of inflation reached 7.7% in 2021, up from 4.5% in 2020. Given the current challenges in accessing food supplies, higher inflation levels could exacerbate the region's food insecurity by reducing consumers' purchasing power while increasing inequality and malnutrition among the most vulnerable groups.

Compounding this threat is the disruption in wheat and other grain supplies from the war-afflicted Ukraine. The Caribbean Region's high dependency on food imports renders it vulnerable to increased food prices, leading to higher levels of domestic inflation.

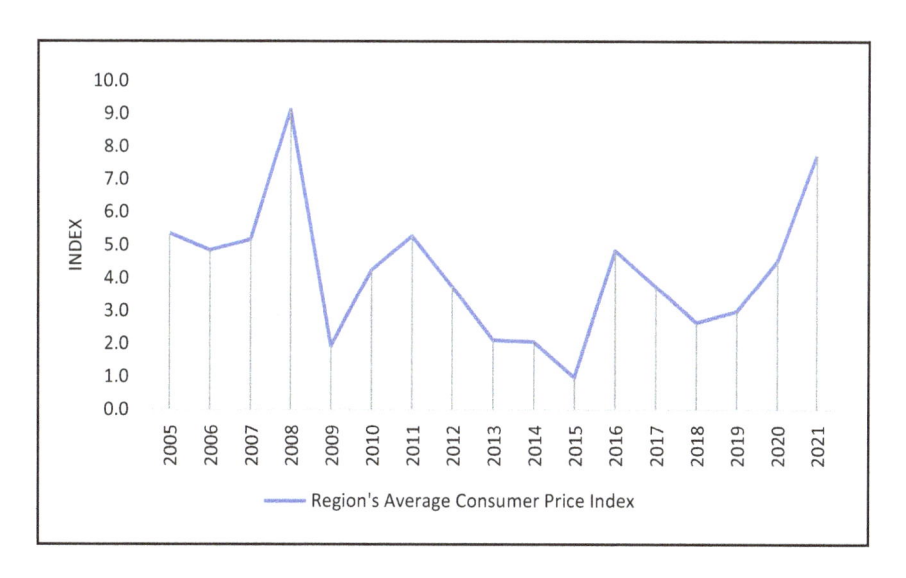

Figure 3.6. Region's average consumer price index from 2005 to 2021.

Source: World Bank Data.

In Suriname, Barbados, Jamaica, and Guyana, food prices increased by 68.3%, 19.9%, 14.8%, and 13.4%, respectively, in 2020 (CARICOM et al., 2022). Furthermore, food consumption patterns have transformed substantially in recent history. These changes can be traced back to increased dependency on imported food, where traditional foods were substituted with imported cereals and stored staples (ECLAC, 2006). Due to the high level of dependency on food imports, maintaining a steady and sustainable supply of food from abroad is crucial for the region. Notably, Ukraine, the latest country to be engulfed by war, is a major producer of cereals.

Food security in the Caribbean Region is likely to deteriorate because of the aftershock of the COVID-19 pandemic, current high-energy costs and supply chain disruptions, lower production levels, and even narrow fiscal space. Furthermore, the recent spikes in fertilizer prices are likely to dampen the region's existing food security challenges. From 2021 to 2022, fertiliser costs increased by almost 82%, adversely affecting food production and prices (Rondinone et al., 2022). Figure 3.7 shows the inflation rates for the selected countries in the Caribbean for 2021 and 2022.

The decline in food supplies is expected to drive up food prices further. In countries such as Guyana, Haiti, and Suriname, food prices have increased significantly between March 2021 and 2022. Specifically, in Suriname, food prices have increased by almost 30% during this period, making it one of the worst-affected countries globally (World Bank, 2022a). Notably, since 2020, Suriname and Haiti have been leading the race with the highest levels of domestic inflation in the region.

High levels of inflation in the Caribbean will likely remain one of the major challenges to many Small Island Developing States (SIDS) because of low levels of diversification and high public debt (see Figure 3.8). Countries that rely heavily on food imports are likely to be affected the most (Boz et al., 2022).

The level of public debt in the region also remains a major concern. Typically, a country's ability to borrow resources to fund its public sector investment programme is contingent on its debt-carrying capacity. As of 2021, several Caribbean countries have exceeded the 64% debt-to-GDP threshold recommended for emerging economies by the World Bank. Based on empirical evidence, if the debt exceeds this recommended

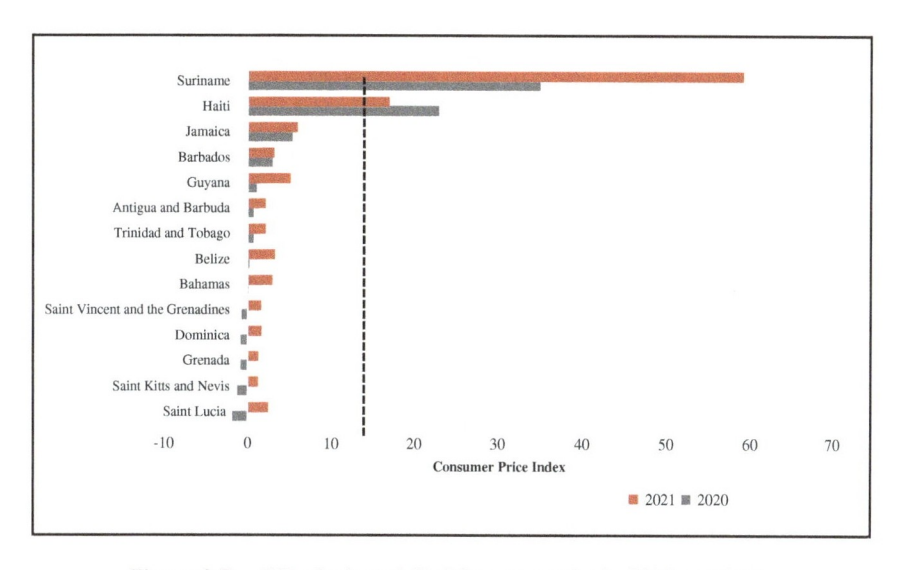

Figure 3.7. CPI of selected Caribbean countries in 2020 and 2021.

Note: The dotted line represents the 2021 average inflation rate.
Source: World Bank Data.

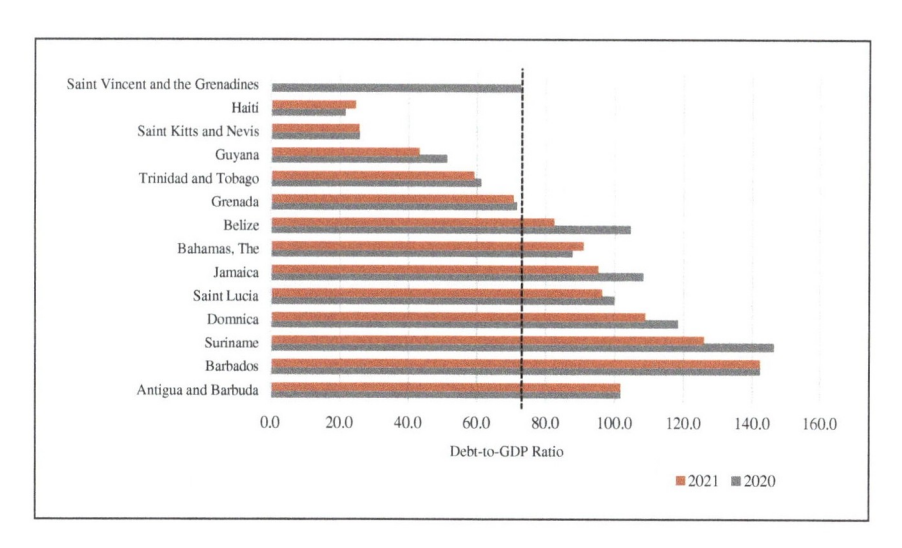

Figure 3.8. Debt-to-GDP ratio in 2020 and 2021 of selected CARICOM member states.

Note: The dotted line represents the sustainable threshold level.
Source: World Bank Data.

threshold, each additional percentage point of debt-to-GDP would reduce real annual growth by 0.02% (Caner *et al.*, 2010).

3.2.3. *Climate change*

The Caribbean Region is considered vulnerable to the impacts of climate change (FAO, 2020). The geographical and demographic characteristics of these countries underpin diseconomies of scale in production, hinder diversification, and decrease competitiveness (Mohammadi *et al.*, 2022). Other climate-related challenges include economic and environmental vulnerability (Sachs *et al.*, 2021). For instance, in 2017, Hurricane Maria inflicted damages to Dominica, which amounted to 226% of gross domestic product (GDP) (World Bank, 2018), while Grenada suffered losses equivalent to 200% of GDP due to Hurricane Ivan in 2004 (Mohammadi *et al.*, 2022).

Achieving sustainable development goals (including ending hunger) in small island developing states, like those in the Caribbean Region, is directly correlated with building climate resilience (Tidemann *et al.*, 2022). However, attaining the latter has proven to be challenging because of population growth, urbanisation, change in consumer food preference, food price volatility, deteriorating terms of trade, etc. (Connell, 2015).

The vulnerability of the region to climate change is shown in Figure 3.9.[3] An increase in the index signifies higher vulnerability. On average, from 2010 to 2014, the region has continuously strengthened its resilience against climate-related events. However, in the years that followed, there has been an upward trend, signifying a deterioration in climate change resilience. In other words, food security in the region became more susceptible to climate-related events from 2014 to 2020, reversing the progress of the preceding half-decade.

Notably, across 2019 and 2020, climate change vulnerability was at its highest in countries, such as Antigua and Barbuda, Saint Kitts and Nevis, Saint Lucia, and Haiti (see Figure 3.10). In the region, climate change has triggered an increase in extreme weather events, such as droughts and high-intensity storms, destroying the region's economies

---

[3] The vulnerability index "measures a country's exposure, sensitivity, and ability to adapt to the negative impact of climate change" (Dame, 2023).

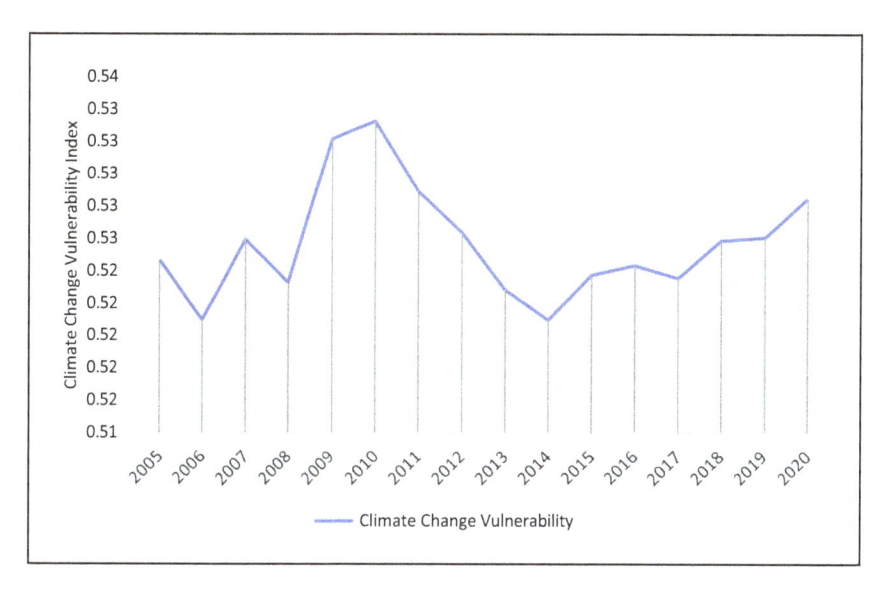

Figure 3.9. Region's average climate change vulnerability index, 2005–2020.

Source: ND-GAIN Data.

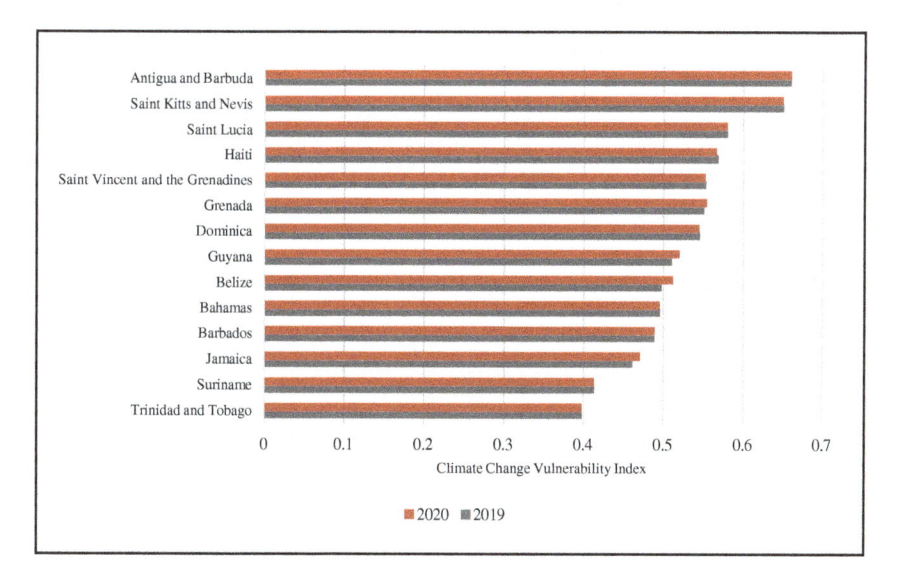

Figure 3.10. Climate change vulnerability index of selected CARICOM member states in 2019 and 2020.

Source: ND-GAIN Data.

and thereby threatening food security (Shultz *et al.*, 2019). For example, in Jamaica, drought tends to affect crop rotation, fruit yield, and freshwater supply (*ibid.*). Similarly, in Dominica, reef species are considered vulnerable to ocean-warming temperatures (Lincoln Lenderking *et al.*, 2021).

Chapter 4

Country Briefs

4.1. Antigua and Barbuda

Table 4.1. Selected macroeconomic indicators: Antigua and Barbuda.

Population (total)	93,219 (2021)
Rural population (% of total pop)	76 (2021)
GDP growth (annual %)	5.3 (2021)
GDP per capita (PP international $)	21,010 (2021)
GDP, PPP (current international $)	1,958,531,520 (2021)
Income level (by per capita GNI)	High income
HDI	0.788 (2021)
	71 out of 191 (2020)
Debt-to-GDP ratio	101.4 % (2021)
Ease of doing business score	60.3 (113 out of 190) (2020)
Moderate or severe food insecurity (%)	33 (2019–2021)
Agriculture as a share of GDP	2.2% (2021)
Inflation, consumer prices (annual %)	2.1 (2021)
Employment in agriculture (% of total employment)	1.8 (2020)
Total land area	0.4 (sq. km thousands)
Total agricultural area (hectares)	20.45 (2020)
Arable land (%)	9.09 (2020)

(*Continued*)

Table 4.1. (*Continued*)

Crop production index	83.83 (2020)
Livestock production index	100.46 (2020)
Cereal production (metric tonnes)	11 (2020)
Food production	32,205,000 (2020)

Source: World Bank Data, FAOSTAT (FAO *et al.*, 2023).

4.1.1. *Overview of the agricultural sector in Antigua and Barbuda*

Antigua and Barbuda's agricultural output consists mainly of vegetables, root crops, a limited range of fruit crops (Caribbean Agri-Business, 2020), and vine and tree fruits (Cooper *et al.*, 2015). Agriculture contributed approximately 2.2% to the country's GDP and accounted for 1.8% of employment in 2020 (World Bank, 2023). Domestic food production in the country is based on local subsistence and small-scale commercial agricultural production (Instituto Interamericano de Cooperacion para la Agricultura, 2019).

4.1.2. *Impact of climate change on Antigua and Barbuda's food production*

Like many Small Island Developing States (SIDS), Antigua and Barbuda is highly vulnerable to the impacts of climate change. The island's location makes it vulnerable to droughts and hurricanes as it sits in an area of the Atlantic that is susceptible to such extreme weather phenomena from June to November each year. In 2020, Antigua and Barbuda ranked 177 out of 189 countries on the ND-GAIN food vulnerability index[1] with a Food score of 0.659, indicating its high susceptibility to the impacts of climate-related events.

---

[1] The ND-GAIN Index summarises a country's vulnerability to climate change and other global challenges in combination with its readiness to improve resilience. It aims to help governments, businesses, and communities better prioritise investments for a more efficient response to the immediate global challenges ahead. An increase in the index signifies an increase in a country's vulnerability to climate change. See more at: https://gain.nd.edu/our-work/country-index/.

Country Briefs 25

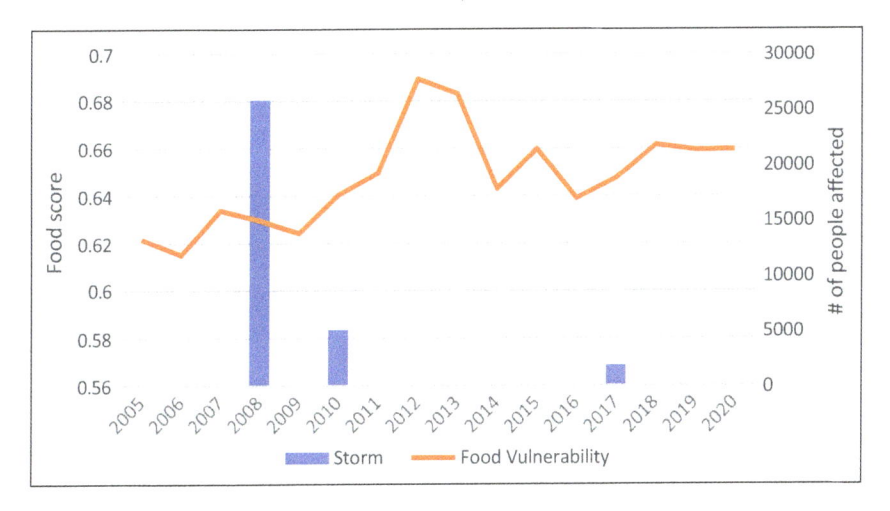

Figure 4.1. Food security vulnerability to climate change impacts (index) and the effect of climate-related events, 2005–2020.

Note: Food vulnerability refers to food security vulnerability to climate change. The axis captures the food security vulnerability index to climate change, while the right shows the number of people affected by climate-related events.
Source: ND-GAIN Data and World Bank Data.

Figure 4.1 shows a marked improvement in the country's food score between 2012 and 2016. This period coincides with the introduction of the country's food security policy. However, from 2016 to 2020, the country's food security vulnerability to climate change deteriorated somewhat. According to the FAO *et al.* (2023), 33% of the country's population faced moderate or severe food insecurity between 2019 and 2021.

4.1.3. *Food production in Antigua and Barbuda*

In 2020, total food production in Antigua and Barbuda rose to US$32.2 million, or 2.35% of nominal GDP, the largest share over the past decade (Figure 4.2). The increase in food production (as a share of nominal GDP) commenced in 2016 and continued until 2017 before a gradual decline in 2018 and 2019, and then an eventual resurgence in 2020 to an all-time high of 2.3%. Notwithstanding the increase in the contribution of food production to GDP, according to FAO *et al.* (2023), approximately 33% of

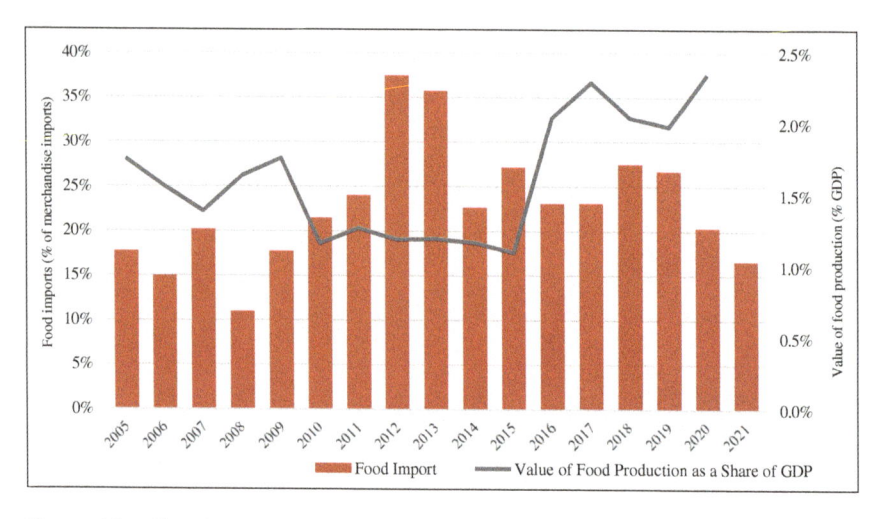

Figure 4.2. Food imports (% of total merchandise imports) and value of food production (% of GDP), 2005–2021.

Note: Food imports represent food imports (% of total merchandise trade).
Source: World Bank Data and FAOSTAT.

the population was faced with moderate or severe food insecurity between 2019 and 2021.

In 2012, Antigua and Barbuda rolled out a Food and Nutrition Security Policy. This policy was introduced primarily to reduce food import bills and lower the economy's dependence on food imports. Since this intervention, the share of food imports declined from 37.3% in 2012 to 16.5% by 2021 (Figure 4.2).

4.1.4. *Investment in agriculture and public debt*

Investment in agriculture has consistently declined since 2005 (Figure 4.3). Private sector investment in agriculture as a share of total domestic credit, an indicator that provides insights into the private sector's role in food production, fell from 0.29% in 2005 to 0.03% in 2019. Holding other things constant, this may potentially lead to an increase in food importation dependency and reversal of the policy dividends from the Food and Nutrition Security Policy in the future.

Compounding this concern is the increase in the debt-to-GDP ratio from 81.3% in 2019 to 101% in 2021. Notably, a higher debt burden could

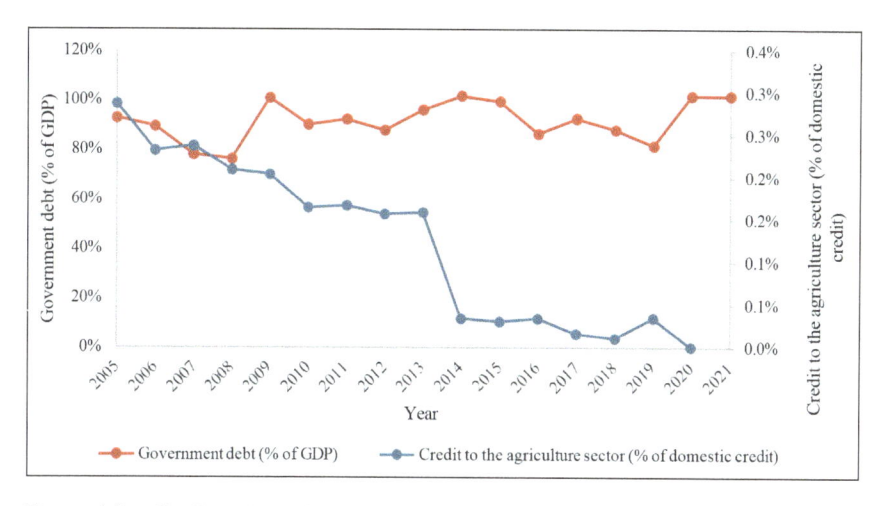

Figure 4.3. Credit to the agriculture sector (as a share of total domestic credit) and government debt, 2005–2021.

Source: FAOSTAT and IMF Data.

reduce access to affordable capital to finance public sector investment in agriculture, potentially leading to higher levels of food insecurity in Antigua and Barbuda.

4.2. The Bahamas

Table 4.2. Selected macroeconomic indicators: The Bahamas.

Population (total)	407,906 (2021)
Rural population (% of total pop)	17 (2021)
GDP growth (annual %)	13.7 (2021)
GDP per capita (PPP international $)	33,188.7 (2021)
GDP, PPP (current international $)	13,537,883,110 (2021)
Income level (by per capita GNI)	High income
HDI	0.812 (2021)
	58 out of 191 (2020)
Ease of doing business score	59.9 (119 out of 190) (2020)
Moderate or severe food insecurity (%)	17.2 (2019–2021)
Agriculture as a share of GDP	0.5% (2021)

(Continued)

Table 4.2. (*Continued*)

Inflation, consumer prices (annual %)	2.9 (2021)
Total land area	10 (sq. km thousands)
Agricultural land (% of land areas)	1.4 (2020)
Arable land (%)	0.8 (2020)
Crop production index	101 (2020)
Livestock production index	100 (2020)
Cereal production (metric tonnes)	643 (2020)

Source: World Bank Data, FAOSTAT (FAO *et al.*, 2023).

4.2.1. *Overview of the agricultural sector in the Bahamas*

Agricultural production in the Bahamas focuses mainly on crop production, poultry, livestock, and dairy, with poultry, winter vegetables, and citrus fruits being the foundation of the agricultural sector. Products such as tomatoes and onions are grown for domestic consumption. While the Bahamas has fertile agricultural land, the country has limited water resources. In 2002, agriculture made up 1.5% of GDP, while in 2021, the sector accounted for only 0.5% of GDP (World Bank, 2023). In 2019, the agriculture sector's share of total employment amounted to 2% of the active population (*ibid*).

4.2.2. *Impact of climate change on the Bahamas' food production*

Rising sea levels associated with global warming threaten the socio-economic activities of the Bahamas since approximately 80% of the country is within 1 m of the mean sea level (The Government of Guyana, 2022). The country is vulnerable to extreme weather events such as hurricanes (*ibid*). In 2020, the Bahamas ranked 110 out of 189 countries on the ND-GAIN food vulnerability index with a food score of 0.495, indicating high vulnerability to the impacts of climate change. The food score, which measures the vulnerability of the country's food production system to climate-related events, showed signs of deterioration over the past 15 years (Figure 4.4). Notably, between 2019 and 2020, approximately 17.2% and 3.4% of the population were affected by moderate or severe food insecurity and severe food insecurity, respectively (FAO *et al.*, 2023).

Country Briefs 29

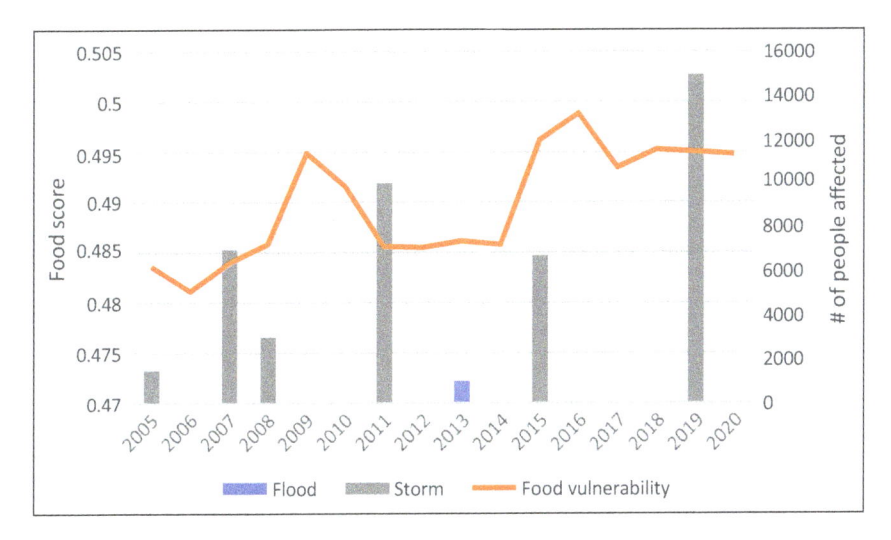

Figure 4.4. Food security vulnerability to climate change impacts (index) and the effect of climate-related events, 2005–2020.

Note: Food vulnerability refers to food security vulnerability to climate change. The axis captures the food security vulnerability index to climate change, while the right shows the number of people affected by climate-related events.
Source: ND-GAIN Data and World Bank Data.

As shown in Figure 4.4, storms appear to have the most devastating effect on people's lives.

4.2.3. *Food imports dependency*

The Bahamas continues to rely heavily on food imports. According to the Commonwealth of the Bahamas (2020), almost 90% of the country's total food consumption is satisfied by imports, of which 80% is from the United States. Figure 4.5 shows that food imports as a share of merchandise imports fluctuated slightly over the period 2005–2021. It peaked in 2020 at about 21% before declining by almost five percentage points in 2021.

4.2.4. *Public debt*

Central government debt as a percentage of GDP in the Bahamas amounted to 90.71% in 2021, an increase of more than 30 percentage

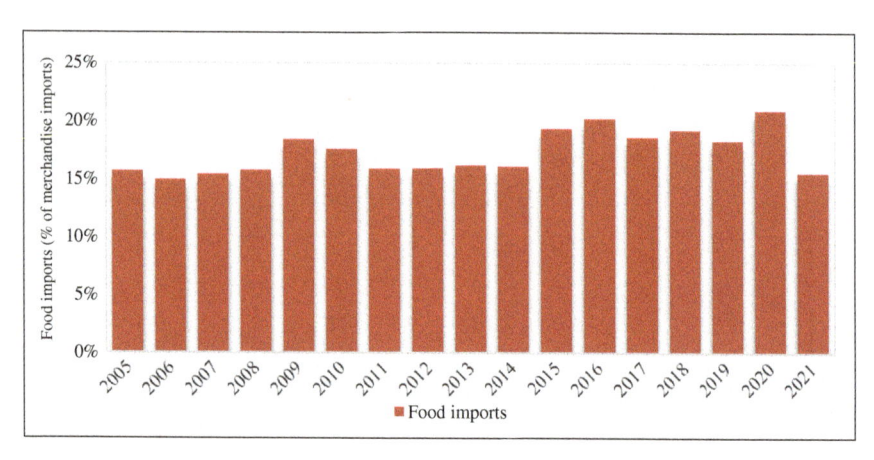

30 *Achieving Global Food Security: The Caribbean Experience and Beyond*

Figure 4.5. Food imports (% of total merchandise imports) and value of food production (% of GDP), 2005–2021.

Note: Food imports represent food imports (% of total merchandise trade).
Source: World Bank Data.

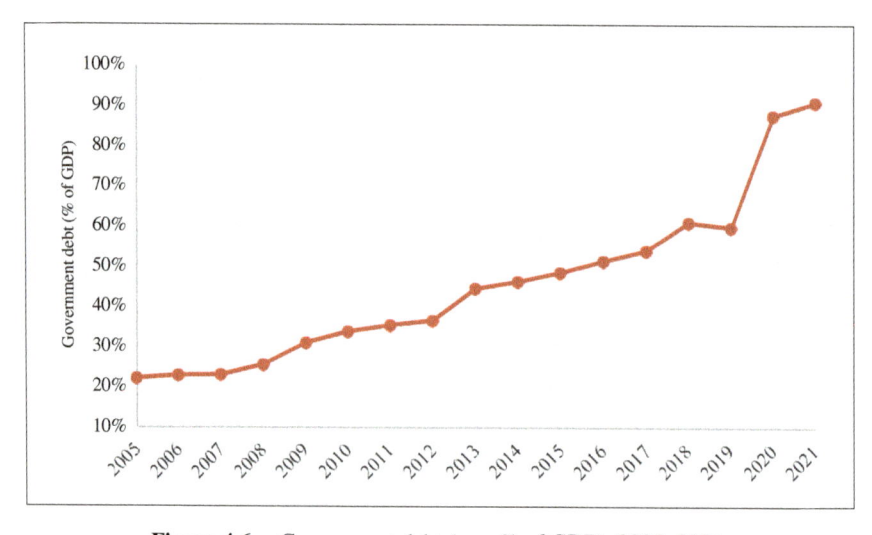

Figure 4.6. Government debt (as a % of GDP), 2005–2021.
Source: IMF Data.

points when compared to 2019, due mainly to, among others, the fallout from the COVID-19 pandemic (Figure 4.6). This suggests some measure of the vulnerability of the country to global shocks. Notably, since the country remains heavily dependent on food imports, narrow fiscal space coupled with higher domestic prices could further weaken the country's food security status.

4.3. Barbados

Table 4.3. Selected macroeconomic indicators: Barbados.

Population (total)	281,200 (2021)
Rural population (% of total pop)	69 (2021)
GDP growth (annual %)	–0.2 (2021)
GDP per capita (PP international $)	15,111 (2021)
GDP, PPP (current international $)	4,249,201,200 (2021)
Income level (by per capita GNI)	High income
HDI	0.790 (2021) 71 out of 191 (2020)
Ease of doing business score	57.9 (128 out of 190) (2020)
Moderate or severe food insecurity (%)	31.1 (2019–2021)
Global competitiveness index	4.2 (2016)
Inflation, consumer prices (annual %)	4.1 (2009)
Land area	0.4 (sq. km thousands)
Agricultural land (% of land areas)	23.26 (2020)
Arable land (%)	16.28 (2020)
Crop production index	92.4 (2020)
Livestock production index	104.2 (2020)
Cereal yield	12 (2020)
Food production	62,910,000 (2020)

Source: World Bank Data, FAOSTAT (FAO *et al.*, 2023).

4.3.1. *Overview of the agricultural sector of Barbados*

According to the Caribbean Agricultural Research and Development Institute, Barbados's main agricultural products are sugar, cotton, vegetables, and livestock. In 2020, food production made up around 1.34% of the country's nominal GDP, up from around 1.14% in 2017 (Figure 4.7). Over the past decade, food imports as a share of merchandise imports trended upwards, moving from 15.1% in 2005 to 23.1% in 2020, suggesting a

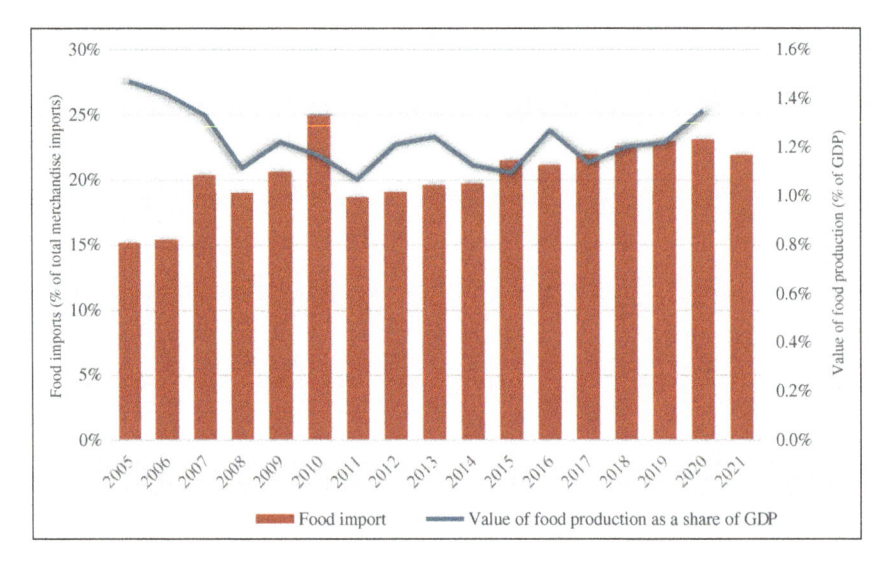

32 *Achieving Global Food Security: The Caribbean Experience and Beyond*

Figure 4.7. Food imports (% of total merchandise imports) and value of food production (% of GDP), 2005–2021.

Note: Food imports represent food imports (% of total merchandise trade).
Source: World Bank Data and FAOSTAT.

higher dependence on imported food (Figure 4.7). However, in the following year, the share of food imports reduced slightly to 21.85%.

4.3.2. *Impact of climate change on food production*

Between 2020 and 2013, Barbados made some progress in strengthening its food security status *viz-a-viz* climate change-related events, as reflected by the decline in the food score during that period (Figure 4.8). However, the vulnerability of the country's food production system to climate-related events deteriorated between 2013 and 2020. With a food score of 0.489 in 2020, Barbados ranked 107 out of 189 countries based on the ND-GAIN food vulnerability index. Additionally, approximately 31.1% and 7.4% of the population were affected by moderate or severe food insecurity and severe food insecurity, respectively, during the period 2019–2021 (FAO *et al.*, 2023).

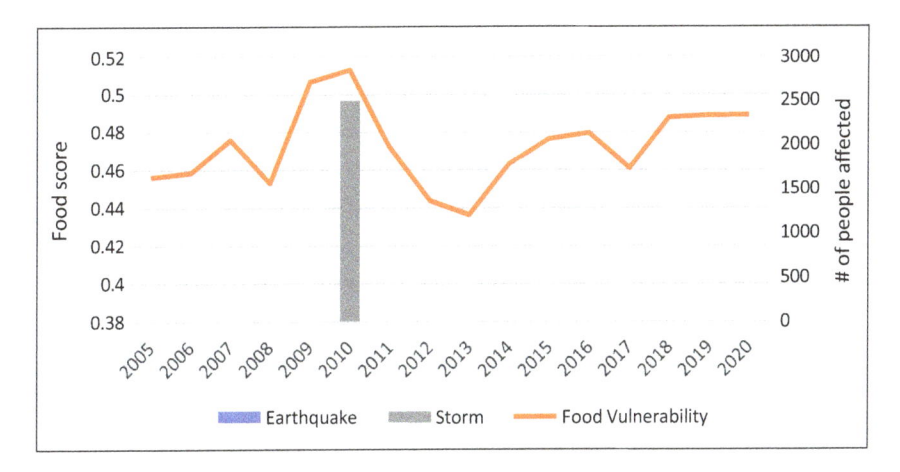

Figure 4.8. Food security vulnerability to climate change impacts (index) and the effect of climate-related events, 2005–2020.

Note: Food vulnerability refers to food security vulnerability to climate change. The axis captures the food security vulnerability index to climate change, while the right shows the number of people affected by climate-related events.
Source: ND-GAIN Data and World Bank Data.

4.3.3. *Investment in agriculture and public debt*

Compounding the concerns of food production vulnerability to climate change, Barbados has seen a sharp decrease in domestic credit allocated to the agriculture sector, with this ratio falling from 1.02% in 2005 to 0.187% in 2021 (Figure 4.9). Lower investments in agriculture could potentially increase dependence on food imports, exposing the country to higher food prices and other adverse external shocks.

Notably, there has been a sharp and persistent increase in the country's debt-to-GDP ratio from 75.2% in 2005 to 141.9% in 2021 (Figure 4.9). One of the main contributory factors to this increase was the fallout from the 2008–2009 financial crisis (Deyal *et al.*, 2019). Interestingly, from 2017 to 2019, the debt-to-GDP ratio fell from around 160% to 120% before trending upward again, mainly due to the advent of the COVID-19 pandemic and other global shocks, including high energy costs (Figure 4.9).

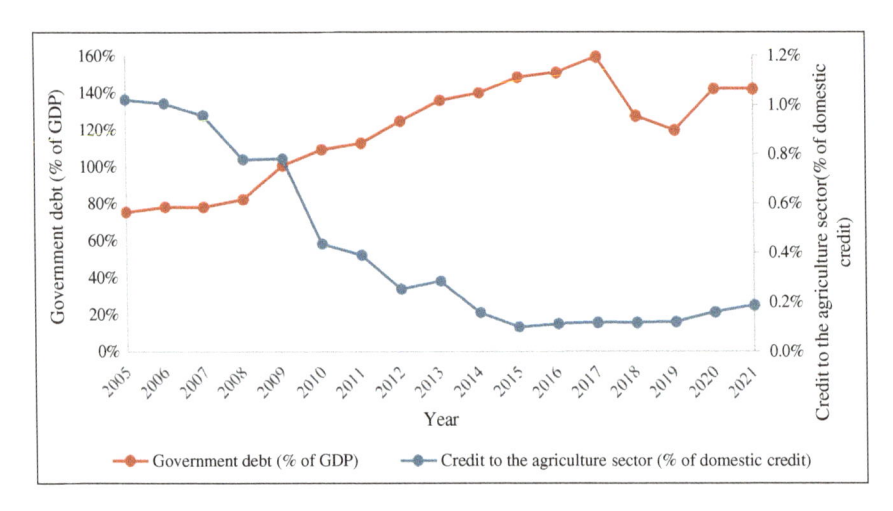

34 *Achieving Global Food Security: The Caribbean Experience and Beyond*

Figure 4.9. Credit to the agriculture sector (as a share of total domestic credit) and government debt, 2005–2021.

Source: IMF Data and FAOSTAT.

4.4. Belize

Table 4.4. Selected macroeconomic indicators: Belize.

Population (total)	400,031 (2021)
Rural population (% of total pop)	54 (2021)
GDP growth (annual %)	15.2 (2021)
GDP per capita (PP international $)	6,626.6 (2021)
GDP, PPP (current international $)	3,850,927,850 (2021)
Income level (by per capita GNI)	Lower middle income
HDI	0.683 (2021) 120 out of 191 (2020)
Ease of doing business score	55.5 (135 out of 190) (2020)
Moderate or severe food insecurity (%)	42.3 (2019–2021)
Inflation, consumer prices (annual %)	3.2 (2021)
Total land area	22.8 (sq. km thousands)

Table 4.4. (*Continued*)

Total agricultural area (hectares)	7.54 (2020)
Arable land (%)	3.95 (2020)
Crop production index	92.8 (2020)
Livestock production index	103.2 (2020)
Cereal yield	112,007 (2020)
Food production	24,806,200 (2020)

Source: World Bank Data, FAOSTAT (FAO *et al.*, 2023).

4.4.1. *Overview of the agricultural sector of Belize*

Food production in Belize has markedly improved during the period 2005–2020 (Figure 4.10). In 2020, the country's food production contributed 11.93% of nominal GDP, the highest in more than 15 years. Interestingly, the country saw a significant upward trend in its food imports as a share of merchandise imports during the same period from 12.2% in 2006 to 20.9% in 2021 (Figure 4.10).

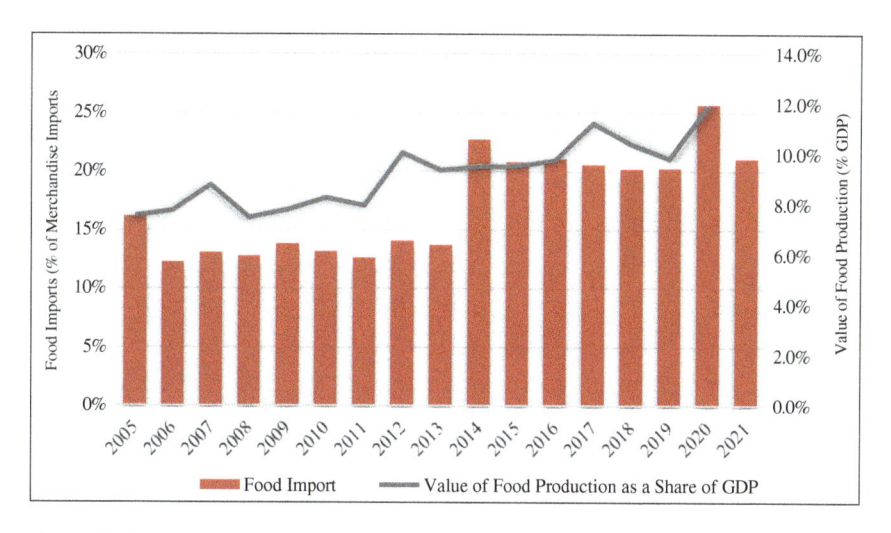

Figure 4.10. Food imports (% of total merchandise imports) and value of food production (% of GDP), 2005–2021.

Note: Food imports represent food imports (% of total merchandise trade).
Source: World Bank Data and FAOSTAT.

4.4.2. *Impact of climate change on food production*

Belize's food score has markedly improved between 2005 and 2013 but gradually deteriorated thereafter (Figure 4.11). The country's food score improved from 0.52 in 2005 to 0.46 in 2013 then regressed to 0.51 by 2020, almost the same level as in 2005. The deterioration of the country's food score during the latter eight years (from 2013 to 2020) indicates an increase in the vulnerability of the country's food production system to climate-related events. In 2020, Belize ranked 115 out of 189 countries on the ND-GAIN Food Vulnerability Food Index. Additionally, 42.3% of the population faced moderate or severe food insecurity during 2019–2021, up from 35.7% during 2017–2019 (FAO *et al.*, 2023). However, while this may be the case, the country has seen a marginal improvement in reducing the proportion of its population experiencing severe food insecurity from 6.1% during 2017–2019 to 6% during 2019–2021. It is also important to note that Belize experienced a sharp increase in inflation in 2022. The

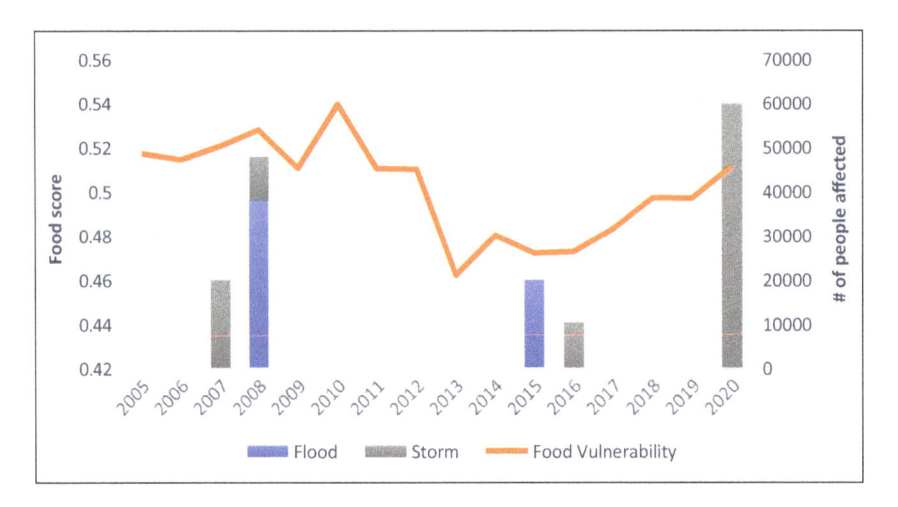

Figure 4.11. Food security vulnerability to climate change impacts (index) and the effect of climate-related events, 2005–2020.

Note: Food vulnerability refers to food security vulnerability to climate change. The axis captures the food security vulnerability index to climate change, while the right shows the number of people affected by climate-related events.
Source: ND-GAIN Data and World Bank Data.

Statistical Institute of Belize (2022) reported a 5.8% increase in consumer prices in April 2022, driven partially by the higher cost of food products, including fresh vegetables, meats, fish and other seafood, and cereal products.

There was an overall contraction in domestic credit to the agriculture sector in Belize. As depicted in Figure 4.12, the share of domestic credit allocated to the agriculture sector fell from around 11.9% in 2017 to 9.5% in 2021. A decline in access to affordable capital for investment in agriculture could have adverse and long-lasting consequences for food security in Belize.

Regarding Belize's indebtedness, since 2014, the country's debt-to-GDP ratio has exhibited an upward trend, moving from 61.53% to a period-high of 104.5% in 2020 (Figure 4.12). While the ratio declined to 82.2% in 2021, it remained significantly above the 2014 level. Belize's high level of indebtedness in recent years could restrict public sector investment in the agriculture sector and potentially worsen food security in the future.

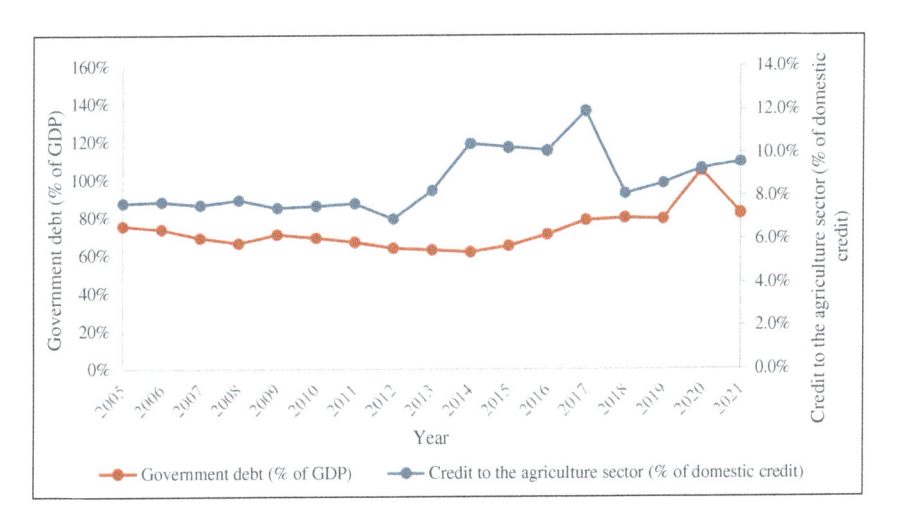

Figure 4.12. Credit to the agriculture sector (as a share of total domestic credit) and government debt, 2005–2021.

Source: FAOSTAT and IMF Data.

4.5. Dominica

Table 4.5. Selected macroeconomic indicators: Dominica.

Population (total)	72,412 (2021)
Rural population (% of total pop)	29 (2021)
GDP growth (annual %)	6.7 (2021)
GDP per capita (PPP international $)	11,950.6 (2021)
GDP, PPP (current international $)	865,363,745 (2021)
Income level (by per capita GNI)	
HDI	0.72 (2021) 106 out of 191 (2020)
Ease of doing business score	60.5 (111 out of 190) (2020)
Moderate or severe food insecurity (%)	Na
Inflation, consumer prices (annual %)	−0.7 (2020)
Total land area	0.8 (sq. km thousands)
Total agricultural area (hectares)	33.33 (2020)
Arable land (%)	8 (2020)
Crop production index	99.2 (2020)
Livestock production index	103.9 (2020)
Cereal yield	193 (2020)

Source: World Bank Data, FAOSTAT (FAO *et al.*, 2023).

4.5.1. *Overview of the agricultural sector of Dominica*

The cultivation of bananas, citrus, coconuts, cocoa, herbal oils, and extracts dominates agricultural production in Dominica. In the past, the country was heavily dependent on banana cultivation. However, the loss of preferential European Union markets for bananas has forced the country to diversify into other crops (non-banana crops). In 2021, the agricultural sector accounted for 17% of the country's GDP (World Bank, 2023).

4.5.2. *Impact of climate change on food production*

Dominica's agricultural sector is highly vulnerable to climate-related events, as reflected in its food score and NG-GAIN food vulnerability index. From 2007, the food score increased from around 0.51 to almost 0.54 in 2020 (Figure 4.13). This increase suggests that the country's food production system has, over time, grown more vulnerable to climate change. In 2020, Dominica ranked 128 out of 189 countries on the NG-GAIN food vulnerability index.

4.5.3. *Food import dependency*

According to the Borgen Project (2020), almost 55% of Dominica's food demand is met by external sources, reflecting a considerable level of reliance on food imports. The country's share of food imports in merchandise imports fluctuated between 2005 and 2020 (Figure 4.14). This ratio increased from 19.4% in 2005 to its peak level of 32.4% in 2013 and then

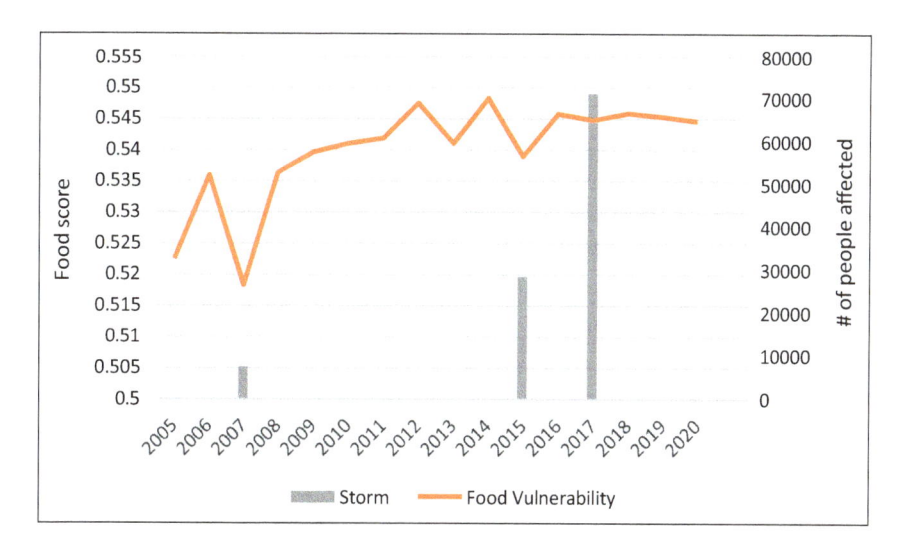

Figure 4.13. Food security vulnerability to climate change impacts (index) and the effect of climate-related events, 2005–2020.

Note: Food vulnerability refers to food security vulnerability to climate change. The axis captures the food security vulnerability index to climate change, while the right shows the number of people affected by climate-related events.
Source: ND-GAIN Data and World Bank Data.

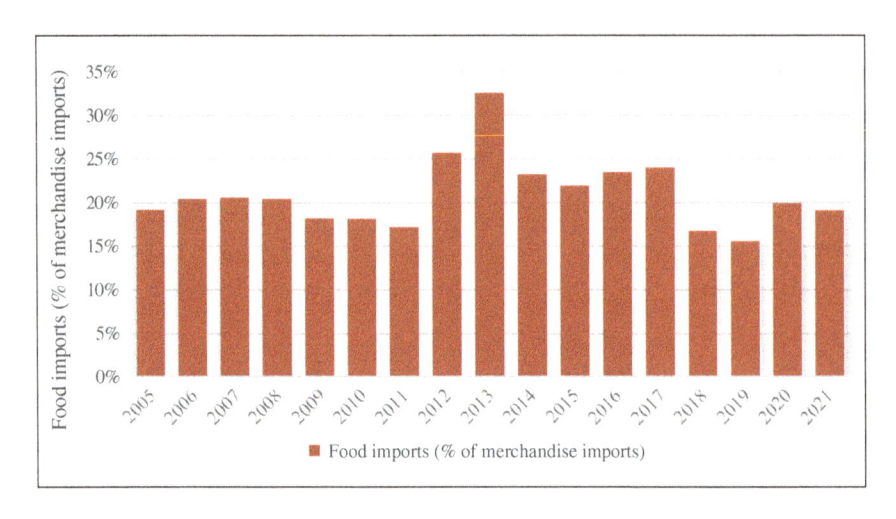

40 *Achieving Global Food Security: The Caribbean Experience and Beyond*

Figure 4.14. Food imports (% of total merchandise imports).[2]
Source: World Bank Data and FAOSTAT.

declined to a period-low of 15.4% in 2019, trending upward thereafter to reach 18.9% by 2021.

4.5.4. *Investment in agriculture and public debt*

Like other countries in the Caribbean, Dominica recorded an increase in its indebtedness following the COVID-19 pandemic, as reflected by the increase in the country's debt-to-GDP ratio between 2019 and 2021 (Figure 4.15). Following the pandemic's onset in 2020, Dominica's debt-to-GDP ratio grew to 118.2%, the highest level over the review period 2005–2021. While the ratio declined to 108.6% in 2021, it remained significantly above all of the other years in the review period except 2020. The recent expansion of the country's debt burden could potentially reduce the ability of the government to invest in resilient infrastructure and other initiatives to support sustainable food production.

It is also noteworthy that the share of domestic credit allocated to agriculture in Dominica contracted sharply from around 1.71% in 2005 to roughly 0.12% in 2019. Given the fallout of the pandemic, narrow fiscal

---

[2] To compute this ratio, merchandise imports were sourced from the World Bank (2023) while data on food imports were sourced from FAOSTAT (2023).

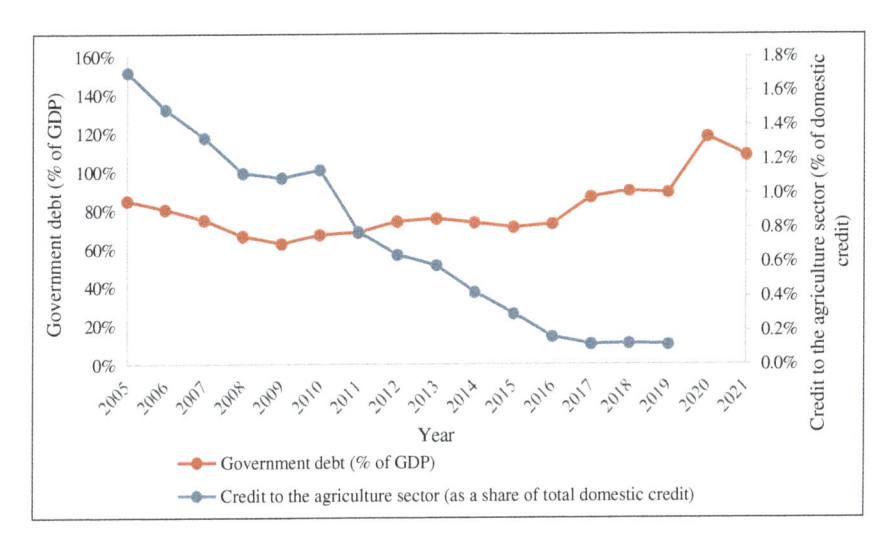

Figure 4.15. Credit to the agriculture sector (as a share of total domestic credit) and government debt, 2005–2021

Source: FAOSTAT and IMF Data.

space, and a small and declining share of domestic credit allocated to agriculture, the country faces significant current and future risks of food insecurity.

4.6. Grenada

Table 4.6. Selected macroeconomic indicators: Grenada.

Population (total)	124,610 (2021)
Rural population (% of total pop)	63 (2021)
GDP growth (annual %)	4.7 (2021)
GDP per capita (PP international $)	15,037.8 (2021)
GDP, PPP (current international $)	1,873,866,430 (2021)
Income level (by per capita GNI)	Upper middle income
HDI	0.795 (2021) 70 out of 191 (2020)
Ease of doing business score	53.4 (146 out 190) (2020)

(Continued)

Table 4.6. (*Continued*)

Moderate or severe food insecurity (%)	22.3 (2019–2021)
Inflation, consumer prices (annual %)	1.2 (2021)
Total land area	0.3 (sq. km thousands)
Total agricultural area (hectares)	23.53 (2020)
Arable land (%)	8.82 (2020)
Crop production index	79.8 (2020)
Livestock production index	147.9 (2020)
Cereal yield	381 (2020)
Food production	72,617,000 (2020)

Source: World Bank Data, FAOSTAT (FAO *et al.*, 2023).

4.6.1. Overview of the agricultural sector of Grenada

According to Grenada's 2012 Agricultural Census, the country's main products include cocoa and nutmeg, fruits, vegetables, and root crops, with minor activity in livestock. Extreme weather is one of the main challenges affecting the country's agricultural production. This may be one of the underlying factors behind the country's recent food score, which suggests the vulnerability of its food production system to climate-related events.

4.6.2. Impact of climate change on food production

According to the ND-Gain food vulnerability index, Grenada ranked 133 out of 189 countries, with a food score of 0.554 in 2020. As shown in Figure 4.16, the country's food score deteriorated between 2007 and 2013 and then improved continuously until 2018. However, a marginal erosion of the recent progress has ensued since then. The country's most recent ranking suggests that its food production industry is relatively vulnerable to climate-related events. Additionally, approximately 22.3% of the population experienced moderate or severe food insecurity during the period 2019–2021 (FAO *et al.*, 2023).

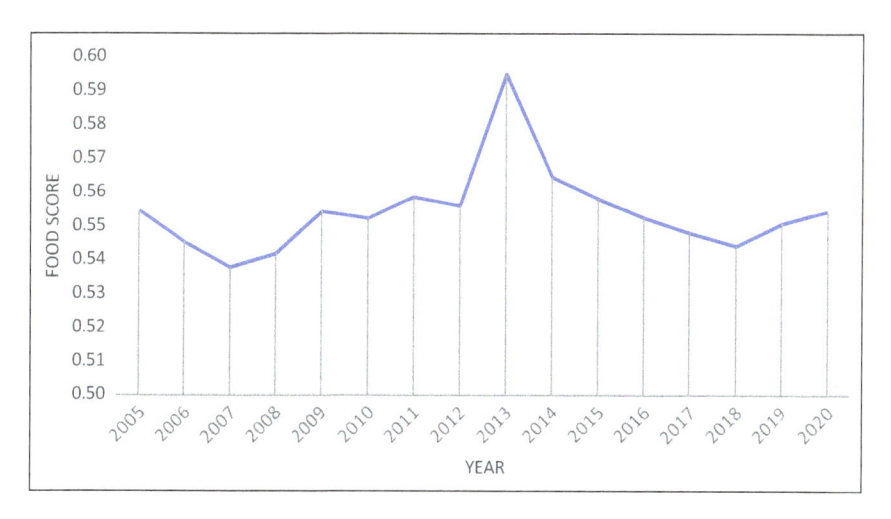

Figure 4.16. Food security vulnerability to climate change impacts, 2005–2020.
Source: ND-GAIN Data.

4.6.3. *Food import dependency*

As shown in Figure 4.17, Grenada's food imports as a percentage of total merchandise imports oscillated between 2005 and 2021. This ratio increased from 16.4% in 2005 to a period-high of 36.7% in 2013. Thereafter, the ratio declined continuously over the next half-decade, reaching 21.2% in 2018 and then finally trending upward until 2021.

4.6.4. *Investment in agriculture and public debt*

Grenada's debt burden has reduced significantly over the last decade, as depicted in Figure 4.18. The country's debt-to-GDP ratio fell from around 105% in 2013 to 59% in 2019. While the ratio has since deteriorated due to the fallout of the pandemic, it remains well below the 2013 level. The share of domestic credit allocated to agriculture also improved from 2005 to 2019. In this regard, the 2019 share of 1.30% represented more than double of the 2005 level.

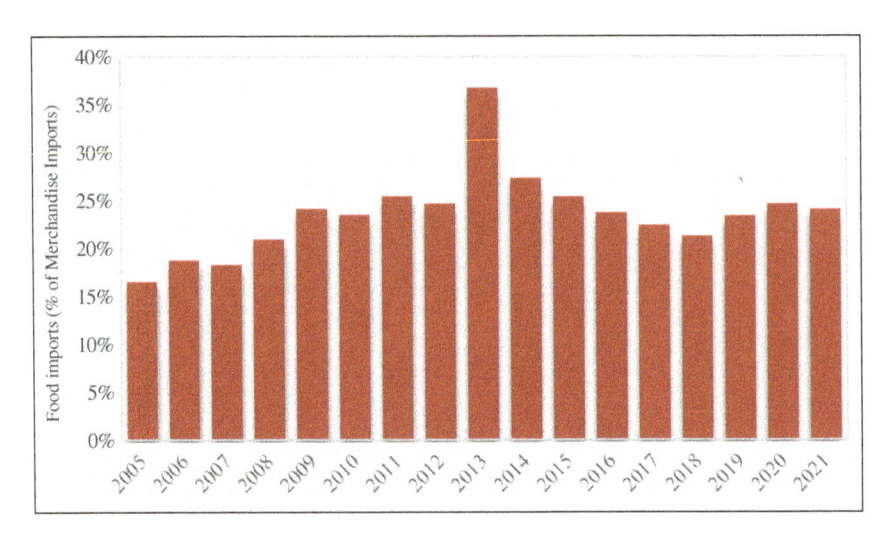

Figure 4.17. Food imports (% of total merchandise imports), 2005–2021.

Source: World Bank Data.

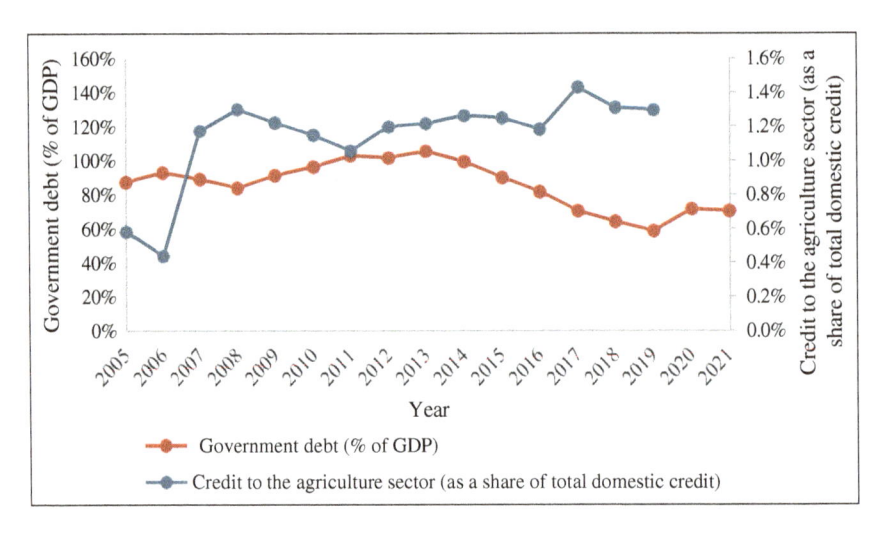

Figure 4.18. Credit to the agriculture sector (as a share of total domestic credit) and government debt, 2005–2021.

Source: FAOSTAT and IMF Data.

4.7. Guyana

Table 4.7. Selected macroeconomic indicators: Guyana.

Population (total)	804,567 (2021)
Rural population (% of total pop)	73 (2021)
GDP growth (annual %)	63.2 (2022)
GDP per capita (PP international $)	14,370 (2022)
GDP, PPP (current international $)	19,379,530,000 (2021)
Income level (by per capita GNI)	Upper middle income
HDI	0.714 (2021) 107 out of 191 (2020)
Debt-to-GDP ratio	42.9 (2021)
Ease of doing business score	55.5 (134 out of 190) (2020)
Moderate or severe food insecurity (%)	na
Global competitiveness index	3.77 (2013)
Agriculture as a share of GDP	13.5 (2021)
Employment in agriculture (% of total employment)	15% (2019)
Inflation, consumer prices (annual %)	5.0 (2021)
Total land area	196.9 (sq. km thousands)
Agricultural area (% of total land area)	6.31 (2020)
Arable land (% of total land area)	2.1 (2020)
Crop production index	109.2 (2020)
Livestock production index	139.5 (2020)
Cereal yield	691,539 (2020)
Food production	667,917,000 (2020)

Source: World Bank Data, FAOSTAT (FAO *et al.*, 2023).

4.7.1. *Overview of the agricultural sector of Guyana*

While there are several large private and public sector farming enterprises in Guyana, agriculture is primarily undertaken by smallholder farmers in both coastal and hinterland regions. The sector comprises the rice industry, the sugar industry, non-traditional crops, livestock, and the fishery sector. The agriculture sector of Guyana is a major export earner and employer. According to the World Bank (2023), this sector accounted for 19% of non-oil GDP and employed approximately 17% of the labour force in 2021.

4.7.2. *Impact of climate change on food production*

Over the past 15 years, Guyana has seen a notable reduction in the vulnerability of its food production system to climate-related events. Figure 4.19 shows that the country's food score has generally been trending downward

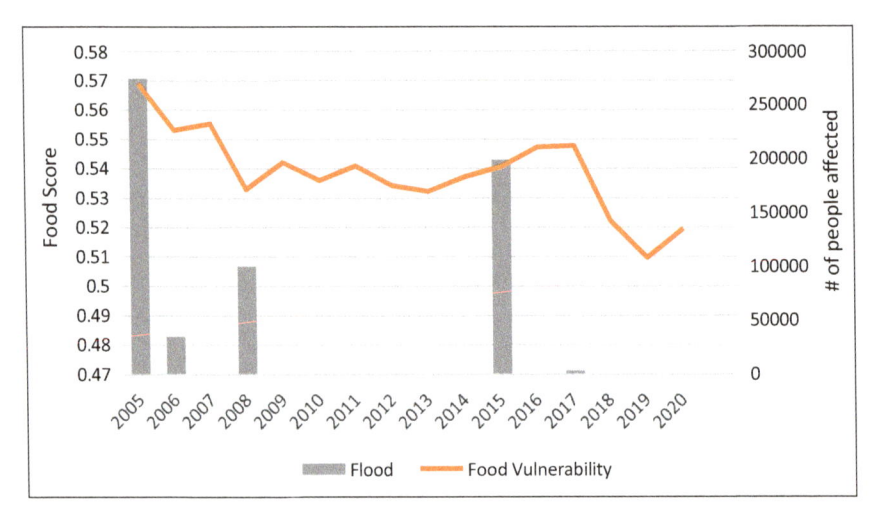

Figure 4.19. Food security vulnerability to climate change impacts (index) and the effect of climate-related events, 2005–2020.

Note: Food vulnerability refers to food security vulnerability to climate change. The axis captures the food security vulnerability index to climate change, while the right shows the number of people affected by climate-related events.
Source: ND-GAIN Data and World Bank Data.

since 2005, moving from 0.57 to around 0.52 by 2020. This implies that the country has significantly strengthened its food production facilities against climate-related events. Based on the food score in 2020, Guyana ranked 123 out of 189 countries on the ND-GAIN food vulnerability index.

4.7.3. *Food import dependency*

Guyana's food imports as a share of total merchandise imports have exhibited a general decline in recent years (Figure 4.20). After maintaining a relatively stable level of between 12% and 15% from 2005 to 2014, this ratio spiked to 17% in 2015, then declined to a period-low of 7% by 2019, and finally increased marginally to reach 9% in 2021.

The contribution of food production to Guyana's GDP has grown exponentially over the last decade, increasing from 2.1% in 2011 to 18.1% in 2018. Despite a decline over the subsequent two-year period, the 2020

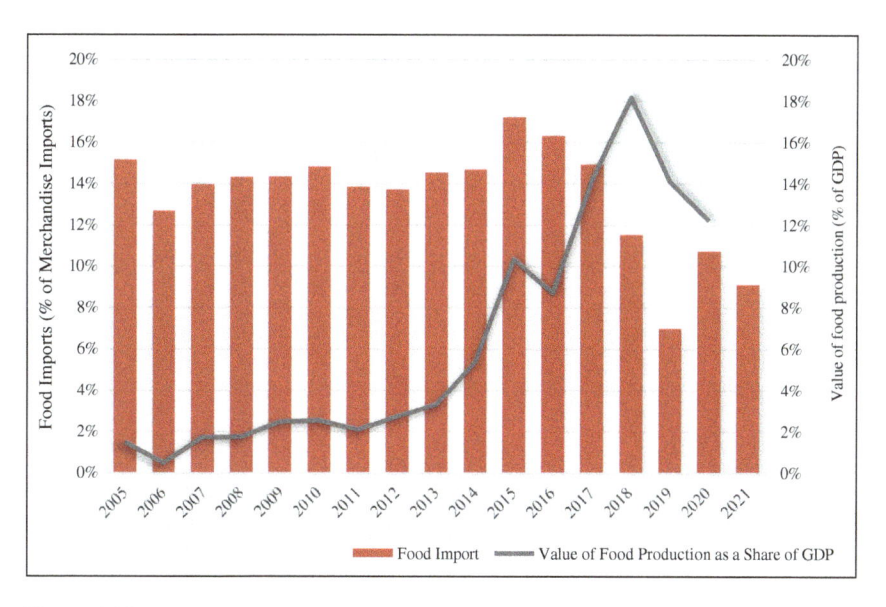

Figure 4.20. Food imports (% of total merchandise imports) and value of food production (% of GDP), 2005–2021.

Note: Food imports represent food imports (% of total merchandise trade).
Source: World Bank and FAOSTAT.

48 *Achieving Global Food Security: The Caribbean Experience and Beyond*

ratio was still almost six times the 2011 level. On the back of this increased prominence of agriculture in the economy, the country has assumed a leading role in CARICOM's initiative to reduce the food import bill of the entire region by 25% by the year 2025 (Vision 25 by 2025). In this regard, several large-scale projects have already been initiated, specifically geared to increase food production, empower farmers, and encourage youth and women participation. Guyana is also collaborating with several CARICOM member states to boost regional food production in line with Vision 25 by 2025 (MoA, 2022).

4.7.4. *Investment in agriculture and public debt*

Since 2005, Guyana has made significant progress in reducing its debt-to-GDP ratio to sustainable levels (Figure 4.21). Between 2005 and 2021, this ratio was more than halved, moving from almost 90.7% to 42.8%. Furthermore, the latest available data show that Guyana's debt-to-GDP ratio at the end of 2022 was 24.6% (MoF, 2023, p. 18). At the same time,

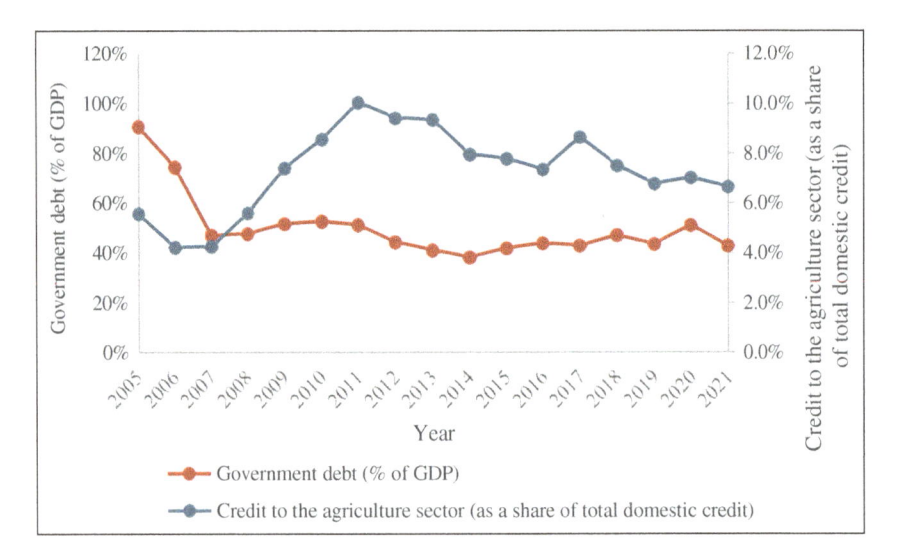

Figure 4.21. Credit to the agriculture sector (as a share of total domestic credit) and government debt, 2005–2021.

Source: FAOSTAT and IMF Data.

the share of private sector investment allocated to agriculture has increased, moving from 5.57% in 2005 to a period-high of 10.05% in 2011. While the ratio has trended downward since then, it remains above the 2005 level. Notably, Guyana intends to utilise the increased fiscal space from a lower debt burden and revenue from oil production and the sale of carbon credits to bolster the resilience of its food production system.

4.8. Haiti

Table 4.8. Selected macroeconomic indicators: Haiti.

Population (total)	11,447,567 (2021)
Rural population (% of total pop)	42 (2021)
GDP per capita (PP international $)	3,153.1
GDP, PPP (current international $)	36,095,639,130 (2021)
Income level (by per capita GNI)	Lower middle income
HDI	0.535 (2021) (162 out of 191) (2020)
Level of development	Developing
Ease of doing business rank	40.7 (179 out of 190) (2020)
Moderate of severe food insecurity	82.5 (2019–2021)
Global competitiveness index	36.3 (138 out of 141) (2019)
Agriculture as a share of GDP	20.62% (2021)
Employment in agriculture (% of total employment)	29 (2019)
Inflation	16.8% (2021)
Total land area	27.6 (sq. km thousands)

(*Continued*)

50 Achieving Global Food Security: The Caribbean Experience and Beyond

Table 4.8. (*Continued*)

Arable land %	38.8% (2020)
Total agricultural area	66.8%
Cereal yield	370,000 (2020)
Crop production index	73.0 (2020)
Livestock production index	99.9 (2020)

Source: World Bank Data, FAOSTAT (FAO *et al.*, 2023).

4.8.1. *Overview of the agricultural sector*

Haiti is considered the poorest country in Latin America and the Caribbean (World Bank, 2022). The country remains one of the most vulnerable to climate change and natural hazards, such as hurricanes, floods, and earthquakes (World Bank Group, 2021). Agriculture and fisheries are considered the largest productive sectors, contributing around 20% to GDP in 2021. The agricultural sector also accounted for approximately 29% of the total employment in Haiti. Some of the country's main agricultural products include cassava, plantains, bananas, corn, sweet potatoes, etc.

4.8.2. *Impact of climate change on food production*

Haiti has historically been extremely vulnerable to hydrometeorological disasters. This may be the case given that the country is situated along a path frequented by Atlantic hurricanes. Other natural disasters, such as landslides, are also common. These climate-related events have had adverse impacts on the agriculture sector in Haiti (GFDRR, 2011).

The vulnerability of Haiti's food production system to climate-related events has receded continuously since 2006, as is reflected in the decline of the country's food score from 0.65 to a period-low of 0.57 in 2020 (Figure 4.22). Notwithstanding, Haiti's ranking of 135 out of 189 countries for 2020 in the ND-GAIN food vulnerability index suggests that climate change remains a major threat to the country's food production system. Moreover, during the period 2019–2021, moderate or severe food insecurity affected 82.5% of Haiti's population, with 45.2% affected by severe food insecurity (FAO *et al.*, 2023). According to FAO *et al.* (2023),

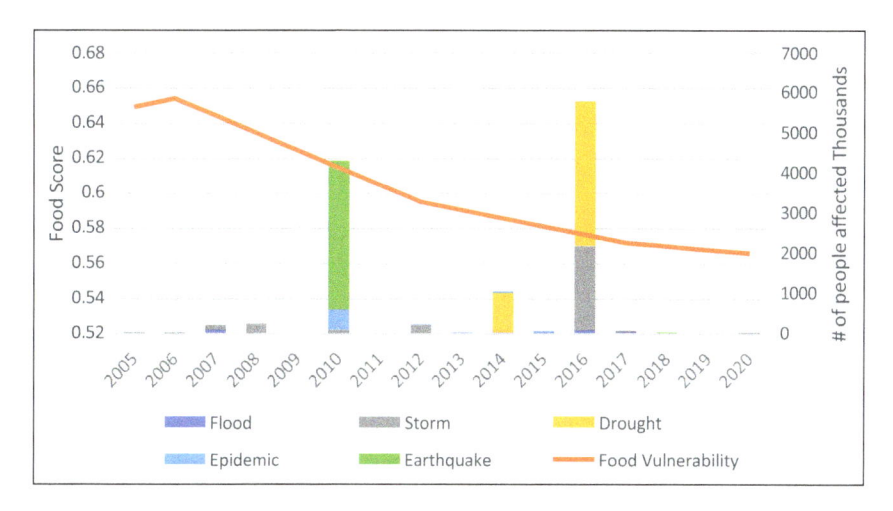

Figure 4.22. Food security vulnerability to climate change impacts (index) and the effect of climate-related events, 2005–2020.

Note: Food vulnerability refers to food security vulnerability to climate change. The axis captures the food security vulnerability index to climate change, while the right shows the number of people affected by climate-related events.
Source: ND-GAIN Data and World Bank Data.

almost 4.7 million Haitians were at risk of acute hunger, of which 1.8 million citizens were in the emergency phase (Integrated Food Security Phase Classification 4).

4.8.3. *Food import dependency*

Haiti imports a significant portion of the agricultural products consumed by its citizens. Furthermore, during the period 2005–2021, the ratio of food imports to merchandise imports for Haiti was significantly above the average ratio for Caribbean countries. Since 2020, this ratio has undergone a spike, exceeding twice the regional average (Figure 4.23). Haiti's high food import dependency may be attributed to urbanization and inadequate agricultural capitalisation. Other factors affecting food dependency include the lack of governmental assistance to local farmers and poor internal infrastructure. These factors have contributed to reduced access to

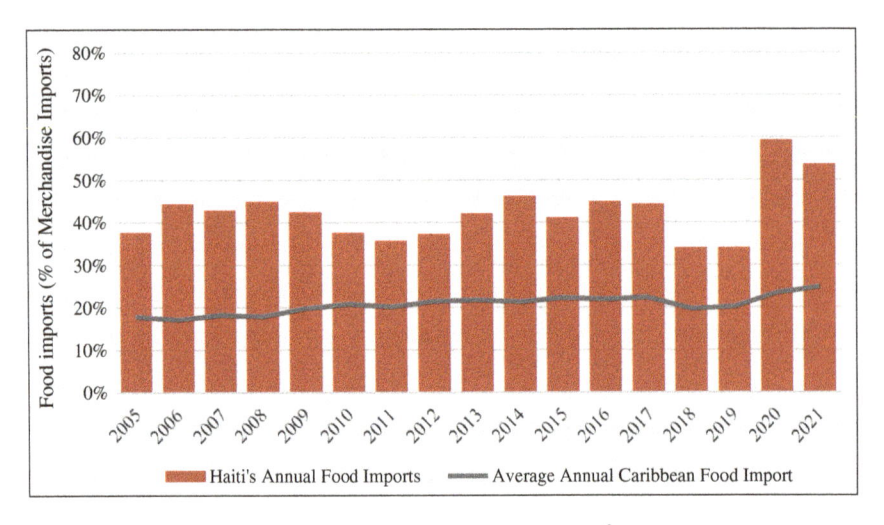

Figure 4.23. Food imports (% of total merchandise imports)[3] and regional average food imports (% of total merchandise imports).

Source: World Bank Data and FAOSTAT.

key means of production, such as capital and adequate infrastructure (De Salvo and Anglade, 2021).[3]

Specifically, between 2018 and 2021, Haiti imported approximately nine million tonnes of food (FAOSTAT, 2022). As shown in Figure 4.23, as a share of the total merchandise trade, Haiti's food imports increased from around 35% in 2019 to almost 60% in 2020 and then declined to 53% in 2021. The country's share of food imports in merchandise imports exceeded the regional average every year during the review period 2005–2021.

Haiti's relatively high dependency on imported food engenders an elevated level of vulnerability to exogenous shocks, with adverse implications for the country's food security. Furthermore, according to the World Bank (2020), while the cost of the average monthly food intake basket in Haiti is affordable, it is not considered "nutritious". In 2019, this basket comprised cereals, pulses, oil, and sugar, representing

---

[3]To compute this variable, food imports (current USD) came from FAOSTAT (2023), while food imports (% of total merchandise imports (current USD)) came from World Bank (2023).

average daily kilocalories of 1,870, with an estimated cost of US$18.57 (*ibid*).

Other challenges affecting food dependency include the lack of governmental assistance to local farmers, poor internal infrastructure, and mobility restrictions instituted during the COVID-19 pandemic. This has led to, among others, reduced access to key means of production, such as capital and adequate infrastructure (De Salvo and Anglade, 2021).

4.8.4. *Investment in agriculture and public debt*

At the macroeconomic level, inadequate public investment in infrastructure to support agriculture undermines strategies geared at minimising the effect of climate change on food production (World Bank, 2013).

Meanwhile, Figure 4.24 shows that Haiti's debt burden has remained relatively stable since 2010 after experiencing a notable decline earlier in the review period (2005–2021). Between 2005 and 2008, the ratio of Haiti's central government debt-to-GDP ranged between 29% and 33%, with the latter year registering a period-high of 32.7%. The largest year-on-year decline for the review period ensued immediately thereafter, with the ratio falling to a period-low of 18.3% in 2009. After rebounding to 23.2% in 2010, Haiti's central government debt-to-GDP ratio fluctuated within the range of 19–26% in the years that followed.

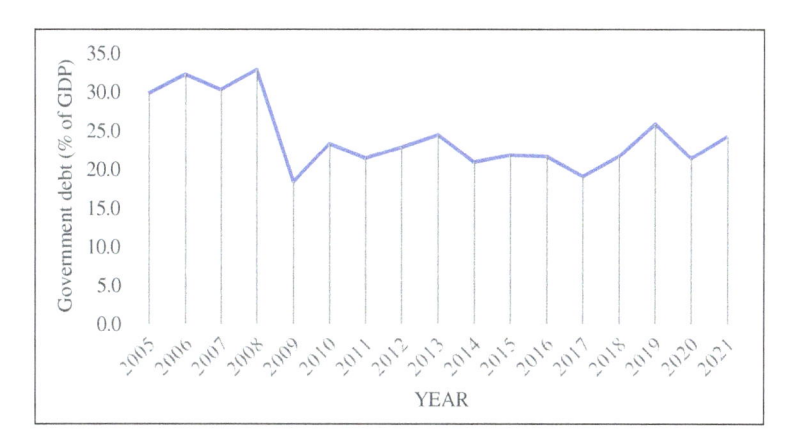

Figure 4.24. Government debt, 2005–2021.

Source: IMF Data.

4.9. Jamaica

Table 4.9. Selected macroeconomic indicators: Jamaica.

Population (total)	2,827,695 (2021)
Population (rural)	43 (2021)
GDP, PPP (current international $)	29,811,646 (2021)
GDP per capita (PP international $)	5,183.6 (2021)
Income level (by per capita GNI)	Upper Middle Income
HDI	0.709 (2021) (110 out of 191) (2020)
Level of development	Developing
Debt-to-GDP ratio	1.06 (2020)
Ease of doing business rank	69.7 (71 out of 190) (2020)
Moderate of severe food insecurity %	50.3 (2019–2021)
Global competitiveness index	58.3
Agriculture as a share of GDP	8.34% (2021)
Employment in agriculture (% of Total employment)	15% (2019)
inflation	5.9% (2021)
Total land area	10.8 (sq. km thousands)
Arable land %	11.1% (2020)
Total agricultural area	41% (2020)
Cereal yield	2,018 (2020)
Crop production index	98.0 (2020)
Livestock production index	104.4 (2020)

Source: World Bank Data, FAOSTAT.

4.9.1. *Overview of the agricultural sector*

The agricultural sector of Jamaica is dualistic: one side (large-scale plantation) produces primarily for the export market, and the other (small-scale) for domestic consumption (FAO, 2013). Agricultural production at the domestic level comprises mainly small-scale farming along the hilly interiors, river valleys, and coastal plains (Clinton Beckford, 2012).

Notwithstanding the relatively small size of the country's agricultural sector and its lack of diversification, agriculture and, by extension, farming remain a major source contributor to national growth and development (FAO, 2013). Some of Jamaica's main agricultural commodities include bananas, coffee, cocoa, and pimento. Recently, efforts have also been made to widen the country's export basket to include milk and other dairy products.

4.9.2. *Impact of climate change on food production*

Climate change remains a major challenge to food production in Jamaica, mainly due to the country's relatively small size, geographical location and fragile ecosystem, and frequency of natural disasters. Extreme climate-related events such as hurricanes, drought, floods, and landslides have severely impacted food production (FAO, 2013). These occurrences have negatively affected farmers' income, employment, and yield levels. New plant-related diseases and pests have also emerged due to the increased frequency of climate-related events (USAID, 2017).

In 2020, Jamaica ranked 99 out of 189 countries on the ND-GAIN food vulnerability index with a score of 0.426, confirming the country's relatively significant vulnerability to climate change. As reported elsewhere, this index "measures a country's exposure, sensitivity and ability to adapt to the negative impact of climate change" (Dame, 2023).[4]

As it relates to the vulnerability of Jamaica's food security to climate change, the county's food score fluctuated between 0.44 and 0.47 over the period 2005–2021 (Figure 4.25). However, a gradual increase has materialised since 2018, leading to a period-high of 0.47 points in 2020.

4.9.3. *Food imports dependency*

While Jamaica remained below the regional average of food imports as a percentage of merchandise imports in 2021, the country imported around US$1.2 billion in food, with approximately 60% destined for hotels, restaurants, and the institutional (HRI) sector (ITA, 2022a).

---

[4] https://gain.nd.edu/our-work/country-index/.

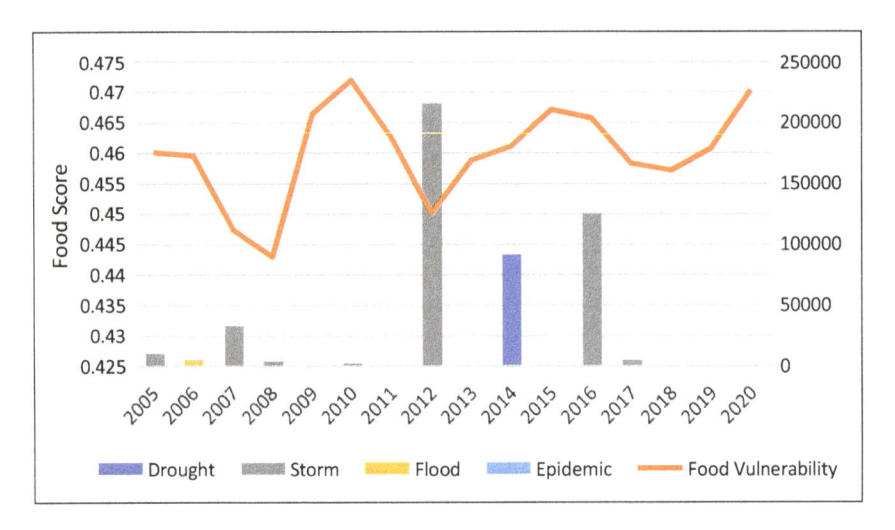

Figure 4.25. Food security vulnerability to climate change impacts (index) and the effect of climate-related events, 2005–2020.

Note: Food vulnerability refers to food security vulnerability to climate change. The axis captures the food security vulnerability index to climate change, while the right shows the number of people affected by climate-related events.
Source: ND-GAIN Data and World Bank Data.

As shown in Figure 4.26, after increasing substantially in 2009, the ratio of food imports to merchandise imports remained relatively stable until 2019. The ratio then spiked to 21.7% in 2021, higher than in each year of the aforementioned period. While the ratio contracted to 20.1% in 2021, it still exceeded the period average for 2009–2019. Notwithstanding the elevated ratios of 2020 and 2021, the country's share of food imports was below the regional average over this two-year period.

On the other hand, food production as a share of GDP in Jamaica exhibited significant volatility from 2005 to 2016, after which a period of relative stability ensued (Figure 4.26). It should also be noted that the country's share of food production trended downward since 2014, moving from almost 16% of the GDP to around 10% in 2019. Despite a marginal rebound in 2020 of approximately 11%, the share of food production to GDP remained significantly below the high of 2014.

During the period 2019–2021, 50.3% of Jamaica's population was affected by moderate or severe food insecurity, with 66.2% of the population being unable to afford a healthy diet in 2020 (FAO *et al.*, 2023).

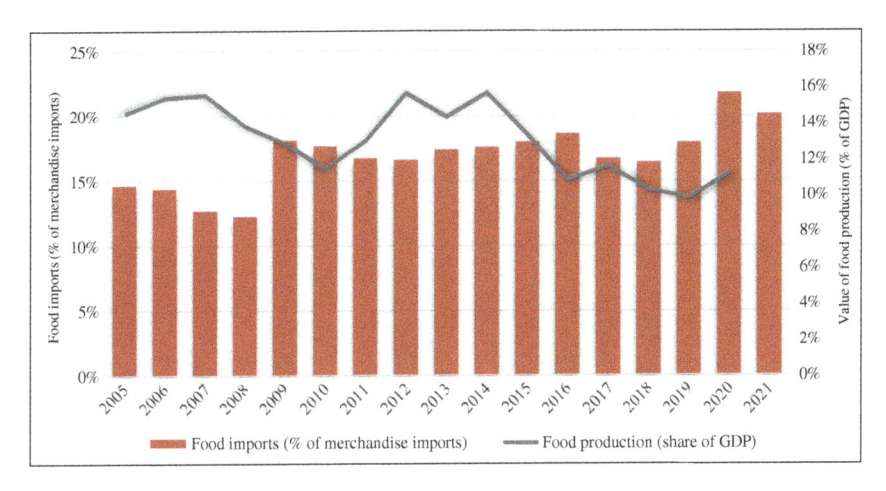

Figure 4.26. Food imports (% of total merchandise imports) and value of food production (% of GDP), 2005–2021.

Note: Food imports represent food imports (% of total merchandise trade).
Source: World Bank Data and FAOSTAT.

4.10. Saint Lucia

Table 4.10. Selected macroeconomic indicators: Saint Lucia.

Population (total)	179,651 (2021)
Rural population (% of total pop)	81 (2021)
GDP, PPP (current international $)	2,574,797.93 (2021)
GDP per capita (PP international $)	14,332.2 (2021)
Income level (by per capita GNI)	Upper Middle Income
HDI	0.715 (2021) (104 out of 191)
Debt-to-GDP ratio	0.45 (2010)
Ease of doing business rank	63.7 (93 out of 190) (2020)
Moderate of severe insecurity (%)	na
Agriculture as a share of GDP	1.8% (2021)
Employment in agriculture (% of Total employment	10% (2019)

(Continued)

Table 4.10. (*Continued*)

Inflation, consumer prices (annual %)	2.4% (2021)
Total land area	0.6 (sq. km thousands)
Arable land %	4.4% (2020)
Total agricultural area	16.3% (2020)
Crop production index	79.5 (2020)
Livestock production index	100.8 (2020)

Source: World Bank Data, FAOSTAT.

4.10.1. *Overview of the agricultural sector*

Agriculture is typically done on a small scale in Saint Lucia, with an average farm size of around 3 acres. A rain-fed system dominates agriculture in this country, and farmers use little to no modern technology (Government of Saint Lucia, 2018). In 2021, the agriculture sector contributed around 2% to GDP while employing a considerable amount of the population (World Bank, 2023).

Saint Lucia is considered one of the largest exporters of bananas in the Caribbean, placing the country at a high risk of export price volatility. Despite a recent contraction in production levels, banana remains the country's top export commodity.

4.10.2. *Impact of climate change on food production*

In recent years, climate change has adversely affected agricultural output in Saint Lucia. These weather-related events include hurricanes, flooding, droughts, and landslides. For instance, Hurricane Tomas in 2010 cost the country almost US$56.9 million. Most of the damages were recorded in the agricultural sector (Government of Saint Lucia, 2018).

At the household level, especially among vulnerable people, there is little or no access to agricultural land. Among rural households, the greatest threat to food security comes from low food production and a lack of support for those who are directly engaged in farming (Government of Saint Lucia, 2013).

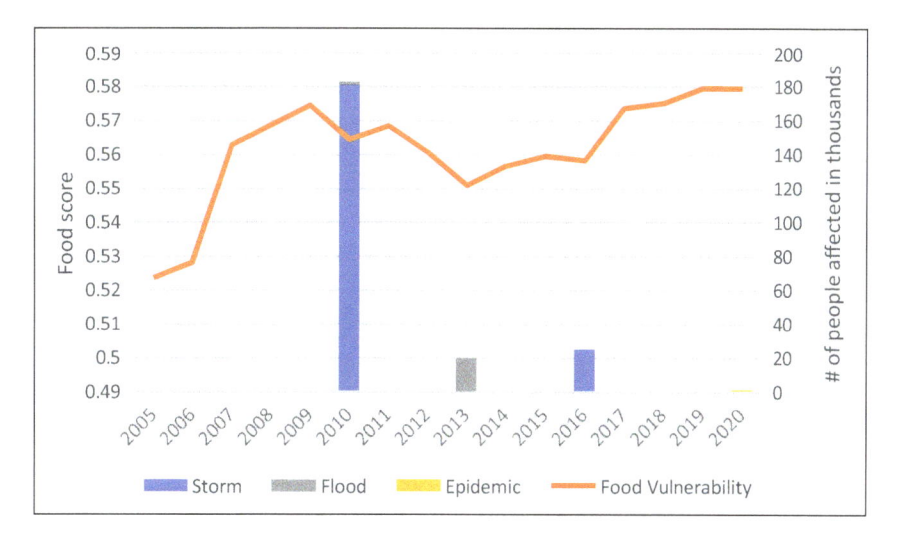

Figure 4.27. Food security vulnerability to climate change impacts (index) and the effect of climate-related events, 2005–2020.

Note: Food vulnerability refers to food security vulnerability to climate change. The axis captures the food security vulnerability index to climate change, while the right shows the number of people affected by climate-related events.
Source: ND-GAIN Data and World Bank Data.

Saint Lucia's food score fluctuated over the 16-year period ending in 2020. In the earliest phase of this review period, the food score trended upward, increasing from 0.52 in 2005 to 0.57 in 2009 (Figure 4.27). This trend then reversed, with the score declining to 0.55 by 2013, after which there was another turnaround, culminating in a period-high score of 0.58 in 2020. The most recent increasing trend of Saint Lucia's food score suggests heightened vulnerability to climate-related events. In this regard, based on its 2020 food score, Saint Lucia was ranked 143 out of 189 countries.

4.10.3. *Food import dependency*

Saint Lucia remains heavily dependent on food imports, mainly processed food (FAO, 2019). The country's annual food import bill amounts to US$4.5 million, a considerable amount of which is spent on importing

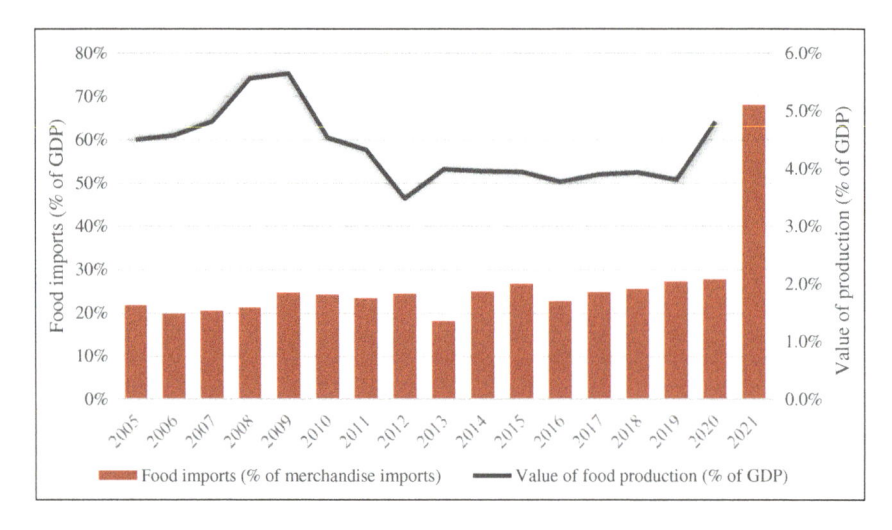

Figure 4.28. Food imports (% of total merchandise imports) and value of food production (% of GDP), 2005–2021.

Source: World Bank Data and FAOSTAT.

fruits and vegetables, including lettuce, watermelon, cantaloupe, and tomatoes (Loop, 2019). Specifically, food imports account for almost 20% of total merchandise imports.

Saint Lucia's annual food imports as a share of merchandise imports were relatively stable during the period 2005–2020 (Figure 4.28). However, in 2021, the ratio spiked to 68%, more than two times the 2020 ratio, which was the second highest during the review period.

4.10.4. *Investment in agriculture and public debt*

Saint Lucia is faced with an inherently low level of private investment in the agricultural sector. This is in addition to the many challenges faced by the sector, including difficulty in accessing land, climate-related impacts,

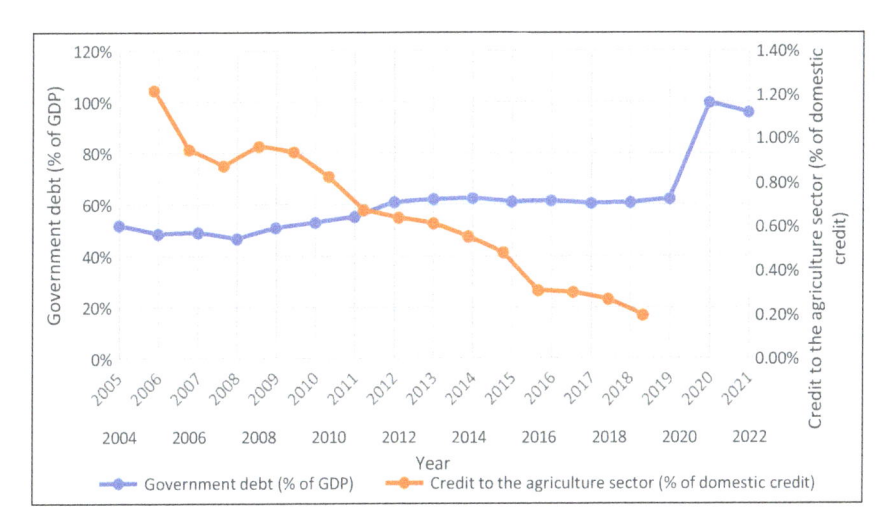

Figure 4.29. Credit to the agriculture sector (as a share of total domestic credit) and government debt, 2005–2021.

Source: FAOSTAT and IMF Data.

the surge in pest and plant-related diseases, and difficulty in accessing capital (Government of Saint Lucia, 2018).

As depicted in Figure 4.29, the share of domestic credit allocated to agriculture displayed a downward trend over the preview period, moving from 1.2% in 2005 to a period-low of 0.2% by 2020. Meanwhile, the debt-to-GDP ratio increased gradually for most of the review period from approximately 52% in 2005 to around 62% in 2019. However, a surge in 2020 made this ratio increase to almost 100%, reflecting the economic fallout from COVID-19 and placing the sustainability of Saint Lucia's debt in a tenuous position. Despite a contraction to 96% in 2021, the country's debt-to-GDP ratio remained concerningly high. This high debt burden may reduce the ability of the government to invest in resilient infrastructure that enhances the productivity of the agriculture sector.

4.11. Saint Kitts and Nevis

Table 4.11. Selected macroeconomic indicators: Saint Kitts and Nevis.

Population (total)	47,606 (2021)
Population (rural)	69 (2021)
GDP, PPP (current international $)	1,385,200.67 (2021)
GDP per capita, PPP (international $)	29,097.2 (2021)
Income level (by per capita GNI)	High Income
HDI	0.777 (2021) (76 out of 191) (2020)
Debt-to-GDP ratio	0.57 (2014)
Ease of doing business rank	54.6 (139 out of 190) (2020)
Moderate of severe insecurity (%)	26.9 (2019–2022)
Agriculture as a share of GDP	1.4% (2021)
Employment in agriculture (% of total employment	0.2% (2001)
inflation	1.196% (2021)
Total land area	0.3 (sq. km thousands)
Arable land %	19.2% (2020)
Total agricultural area	23.1% (2021)
Crop production index	101.7
Livestock production index	66.0

Source: World Bank Data, FAOSTAT.

4.11.1. *Overview of the agricultural sector*

The agricultural sector of Saint Kitts and Nevis comprises mainly rain-fed small-scale farms with an average size of 1 hectare. These farms cultivate ground provision and vegetables. However, there are large-scale commercial farms (more than 5 hectares) that focus on exports, such as bananas, plantains, coconuts, and citrus (OECS, 2021).

In 2021, the agriculture sector contributed approximately 1.2% to GDP. The sector also accounted for 0.2% of total employment during that year. Despite this relatively small share, agriculture has the potential to become a major contributor to the country's economic growth. For instance, during the 2002 economic recession and the 2008 financial crisis, the agricultural sector recorded positive and significant growth rates during these periods.

4.11.2. *Impact of climate change on food production*

Food production in Saint Kitts and Nevis is vulnerable to climate change-related events. Rising sea levels and extreme weather events tend to affect aquatic habitats and fish species. These changes are likely to compound other threats to the sector, such as overfishing, pollution, and the proliferation of invasive species (OECS, 2021).

Saint Kitts and Nevis' vulnerability to climate change is affirmed by its ranking of 175 out of 189 countries on the ND-GAIN food vulnerability index. Over the review period 2005–2020, the country's food score exhibited a fluctuating trend but experienced an overall increase from 0.62 in 2005 to 0.65 in 2020, suggesting an escalation in its exposure to the adverse effects of climate-related events (Figure 4.30).

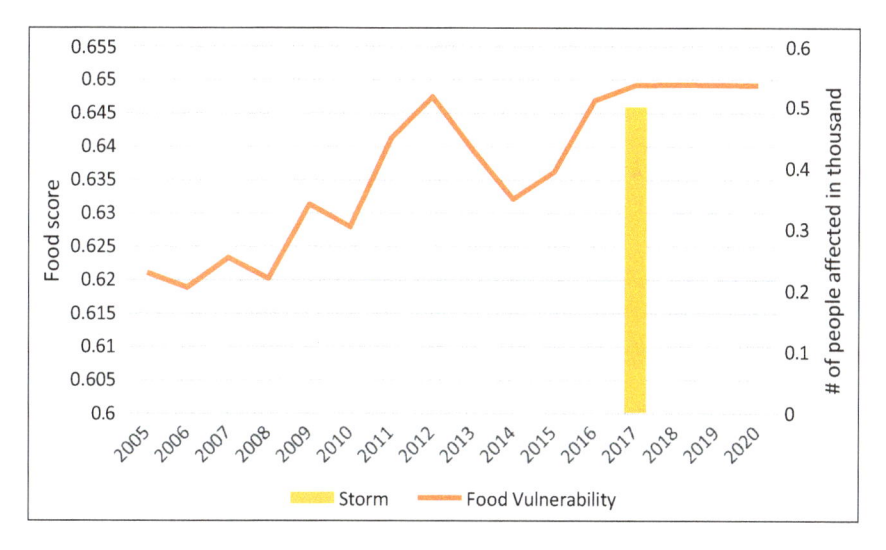

Figure 4.30. Food security vulnerability to climate change impacts (index) and the effect of climate-related events, 2005–2020.

Note: Food vulnerability refers to food security vulnerability to climate change. The axis captures the food security vulnerability index to climate change, while the right shows the number of people affected by climate-related events.
Source: ND-GAIN Data and World Bank Data.

4.11.3. Food import dependency

Saint Kitts and Nevis is considered a net food importer. This may be the case given the country's inherent challenges of low food productivity, an inadequate irrigation system, short-term land tenures, difficulty accessing affordable capital, and overfishing.

Food imports as a share of merchandise imports fluctuated between 18% and 26% during the period 2005–2017 but increased in each of the last four years for which data are available. In 2021, food imports accounted for around 17% of total merchandise imports, almost 7% lower than the regional average of 25%. This represents a marginal increase of about 2% when compared to 2019. Notably, in 2022, the country's food import bill stood at US$140 million (Caricom Today, 2022b).

As is evident in Figure 4.31, food production as a share of GDP was relatively stable from 2015 to 2019, ranging from around 1.0 to 1.1%, and

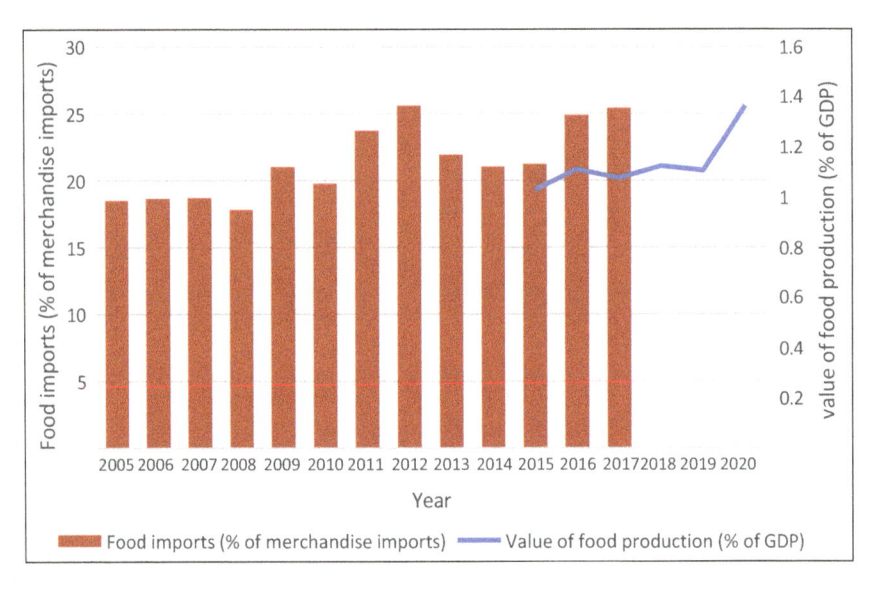

Figure 4.31. Food imports (% of total merchandise imports) and value of food production (% of GDP), 2005–2021.

Note: Food imports represent food imports (% of total merchandise trade).
Source: World Bank Data and FAOSTAT.

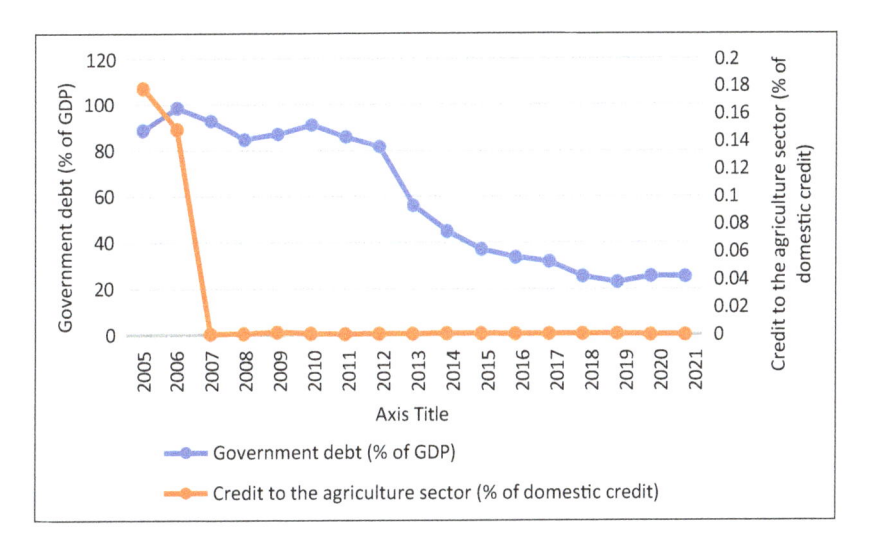

Figure 4.32. Credit to the agriculture sector (as a share of total domestic credit) and government debt, 2005–2021.

Source: FAOSTAT and IMF Data.

then spiked to 1.4% in 2020. The overall pattern seems to suggest the presence of a relatively low level of food production in Saint Kitts and Nevis.

As shown in Figure 4.32, the debt burden of Saint Kitts and Nevis has reduced substantially from 2005 to 2021. After peaking at 98.5% in 2006, the debt-to-GDP ratio exhibited a consistent downward trend, reaching a period-low of 22.8% in 2019. The ratio has since shown a margin rebound to 25.3% at the end of 2021 but remains almost four times lower than in 2006. The country's improved debt sustainability position implies expanded fiscal space to invest in initiatives that promote enhanced food insecurity. This may compensate for the limited private sector investment in the agriculture sector, which is less than 1% of the domestic credit (Figure 4.32). In essence, less than one cent of every dollar of domestic credit went to the agricultural sector. This corroborates earlier claims of difficulty in accessing domestic credit for agricultural investment.

4.12. Saint Vincent and the Grenadines

Table 4.12. Selected macroeconomic indicators: Saint Vincent and Grenadines.

Population (total)	104,332 (2021)
Population (rural)	47 (2021)
GDP, PPP (current international $)	1,569,706.42 (2021)
GDP per capita, PPP (international $)	15,045.3 (2021)
Income level (by per capita GNI)	Upper Middle Income
HDI	0.751 (2021)
	82 out of 191 (2021)
Level of development	Developing
Debt-to-GDP ratio	0.53 (2009)
Ease of doing business rank	57.1 (130 out of 190) (2020)
Moderate of severe insecurity (%)	33.3 (2019–2021)
Agriculture as a share of GDP	6.9% (2021)
Employment in agriculture (% of total employment	10 % (2020)
Inflation, consumer prices (annual %)	1.6% (2021)
Total land area	0.4 (sq. km thousands)
Arable land %	5.1% (2020)
Total agricultural area	17.9% (2020)
Cereal yield	848 (2020)
Crop production index	106.8 (2020)
Livestock production index	95.4 (2020)

Source: World Bank Data, FAOSTAT.

4.12.1. *Overview of the agricultural sector*

The agriculture sector in Saint Vincent and the Grenadines consists mainly of small farmers due to the island nation's mountainous terrain. The country has around 8,000 small farmers and 1,500 fisherfolks (IICA, 2022). During the 1980s and 1990s, the country exported mainly bananas and root crops, which jointly contributed around 19% of annual GDP. However, since the removal of the European Union's preferential market access arrangements, banana exports fell from about 38,947 metric tons in 1998 to a mere 8,937 metric tons in 2010.

Agriculture has nonetheless remained one of the largest sources of employment in Saint Vincent and the Grenadines. Presently, efforts are underway to help diversify the country's crop production to include coconuts and other root crops (Caribbean Agribusiness, 2022a).

4.12.2. *Impact of climate change on food production*

The effect of climate change on Saint Vincent and the Grenadines is well documented. For instance, a drought over the period 2008–2009, along with Hurricane Tomas in 2010 and heavy rainfall in 2011, collectively cost the country around 25% of its GDP. Notably, agriculture and, by extension, farmers were affected the most (Government of Saint Vincent and the Grenadines, 2011).

Between 2005 and 2020, Saint Vincent and the Grenadines' food score was characterised by an initial upward climb, followed by relative stability. The country's food score climbed from a period-low of 0.51 in 2006 to 0.55 by 2011 (Figure 4.33). The above-mentioned period of stability ensued thereafter, during which the score hovered between 0.55 and 0.56. This implies that while the country's food production system has

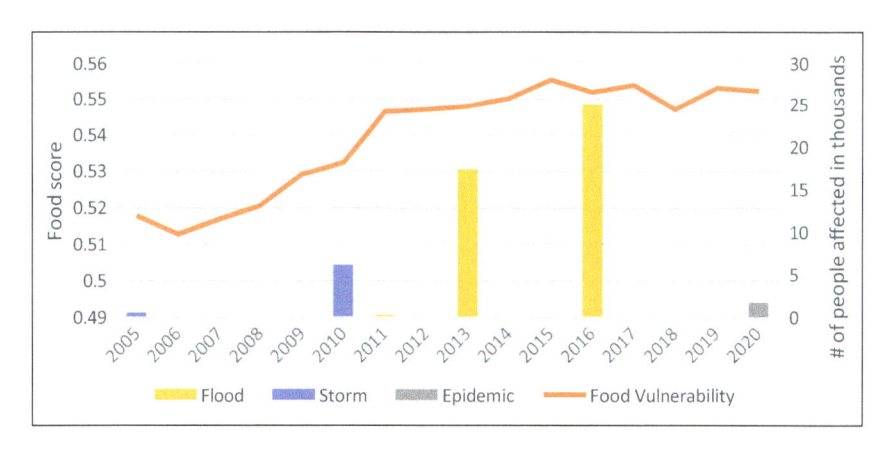

Figure 4.33. Food security vulnerability to climate change Impacts (index) and the effect of climate-related events, 2005–2020.

Note: Food vulnerability refers to food security vulnerability to climate change. The axis captures the food security vulnerability index to climate change, while the right shows the number of people affected by climate-related events.

Source: ND-GAIN Data and World Bank Data.

become more vulnerable to climate-related events over the past 14 years, vulnerabilities have stabilised in recent years. The country was ranked 132 out of 189 countries based on its recent food score.

According to the FAO *et al.* (2023), approximately 33.3% of the population of Saint Vincent and the Grenadines was affected by moderate or severe food insecurity during the period 2019–2021, while 10.3% was affected by severe food insecurity.

4.12.3. *Food import dependency*

Saint Vincent and the Grenadines continues to rely heavily on food imports to satisfy domestic demand. The decline in banana exports to Britain and the European Union due to the removal of preferential trade arrangements has led to a significant decline in the country's foreign exchange earnings. Furthermore, fluctuations in global food prices and other exogenous variables have further deteriorated the country's food security status.

As shown in Figure 4.34, the share of food imports in merchandise imports has generally trended upwards from 2005 to 2021. Between 2005

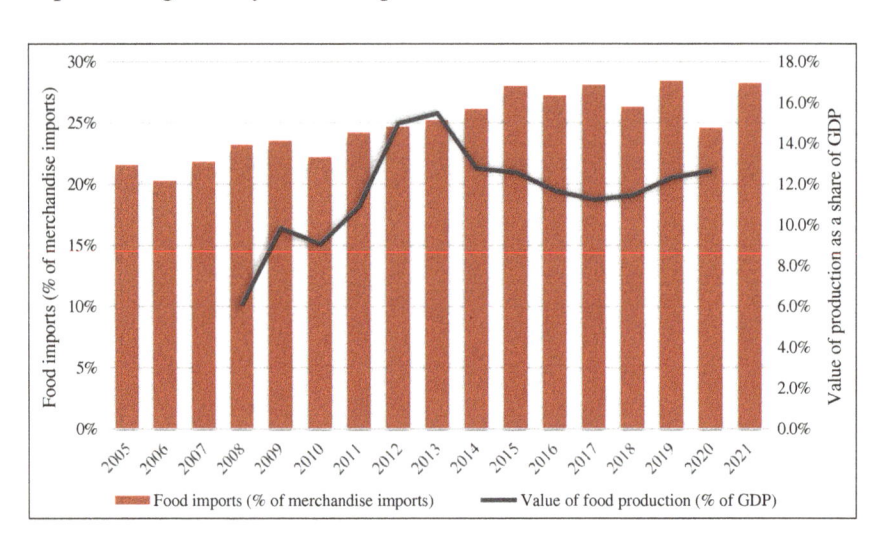

Figure 4.34. Food imports (% of total merchandise imports) and value of food production (% of GDP), 2005–2021.

Note: Food imports represent food imports (% of total merchandise trade).
Source: World Bank (2023) and FAOSTAT (2023).

and 2012, this ratio never exceeded 25%. Conversely, from 2013 to 2021, the share of food imports in merchandise imports exceeded 25% in every year except 2020, during which the ratio fell below the 25% mark by a mere 0.6%.

4.12.4. *Investment in agriculture and public debt*

Investment in the agricultural sector of Saint Vincent and the Grenadines has traditionally been low and sub-optimal due to a lack of access to affordable capital. Compounding this dilemma is the unavailability of applied technology, limited access to human resources and a lack of market opportunities, and relatively low levels of public sector investment in critical infrastructure geared at mitigating the harmful effects of climate-related events (Government of Saint Vincent and the Grenadines, 2011).

As depicted in Figure 4.35, the share of domestic credit allocated to agriculture in Saint Vincent and the Grenadines hovered around 1.1 and 1.3% between 2005 and 2008 and then declined appreciably thereafter, never exceeding 0.2% between 2009 and 2019. Meanwhile, the country's debt-to-GDP ratio exhibited a generally increasing pattern for most of the review period from about 36.9% in 2006 to 65% by 2016. Though there

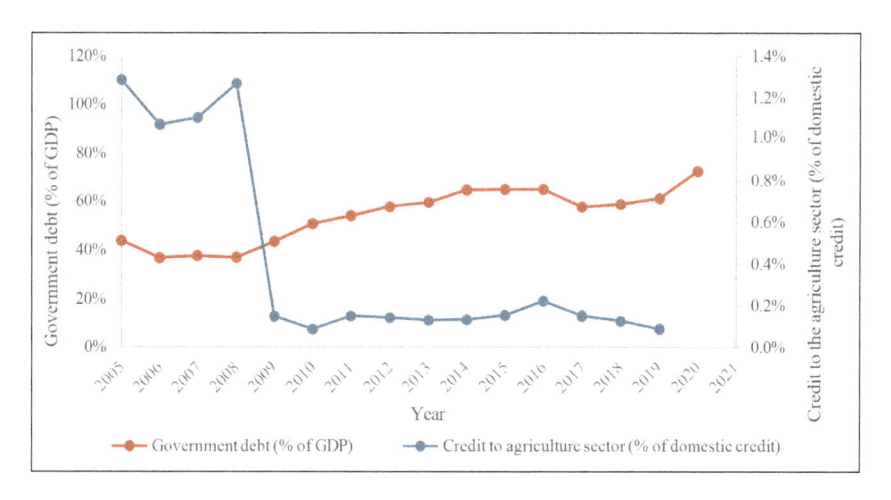

Figure 4.35. Credit to the agriculture sector (as a share of total domestic credit) and government debt, 2005–2021.

Source: FAOSTAT and IMF Data.

was a slight decline to 57.8% in 2017, the upward trajectory then resumed, culminating at a period-high of 72% in 2020. The increasing debt burden, coupled with limited allocation of domestic credit to the agriculture sector, could potentially expose Saint Vincent and the Grenadines to elevated levels of food insecurity in the future.

4.13. Suriname

Table 4.13. Selected macroeconomic indicators: Suriname.

Population (total)	612,985 (2021)
Population (rural)	34 (2021)
GDP, PPP (current international $)	9,944,256.86 (2021)
GDP per capita, PPP (international $)	16,222.7 (2021)
Income level (by per capita GNI)	Upper middle income
HDI	0.73 (2021) (92 out of 191) (2020)
Level of development	Developing
Ease of doing business rank	47.5 (162 out of 190) (2020)
Moderate of Severe Insecurity (%)	35.8 (2019–2021)
Global competitiveness index	3.75 (2013)
Agriculture as a share of GDP	9.2% (2021)
Employment in agriculture (% of Total employment)	8% (2020)
Inflation, consumer prices (annual %)	59.1% (2021)
Total land area	156.0 (sq. km thousands)
Arable land %	0.4% (2020)
Total agricultural area	0.538% (2020)

Table 4.13. (*Continued*)

Crop production index	97.9 (2020)
Livestock production index	108.7 (2020)
Cereal production (metric tonnes)	285,858

Source: World Bank Data, FAOSTAT.

4.13.1. *Overview of the agricultural sector*

Suriname's agricultural produce consists primarily of rice, bananas, poultry, and cattle. The sector employs around 17% of the country's labour force. Most farms are of small scale, and employment is seasonal (GCF, 2020). The agricultural sector plays a significant role in the country's economy, generating at least 5% of total foreign exchange, and is responsible for producing the country's leading staple food, rice (Caribbean Agribusiness, 2022b).

Rice and bananas, two of the top agricultural exports of Suriname, increased from US$69 million in 2007 to US$115 million in 2011 (Caribbean Agribusiness, 2022b). Export earnings from bananas exceeded that of all other food items produced by Suriname, with the largest domestic producer of this fruit being a state-owned enterprise.

4.13.2. *Impact of climate change on food production*

The susceptibility of Suriname's food production system to the negative effects of climate-related events is reflected in Figure 4.36, which shows the evolution of the country's food score for the period 2005–2020. As reflected in Figure 4.36, the country's food score fluctuated during the period 2005–2017, declining from a period-high of 0.42 in 2005 to a period-low of 0.39 in 2006 and then varying between 0.39 and 0.41 until 2018. Since then, the country's food score has stabilised at 0.41. With the recent food score, Suriname was ranked 72 out of 189 countries on the ND-GAIN food vulnerability index.

Other challenges plaguing the country's agricultural sector include poor irrigation and drainage systems, rising sea levels, and lack of access to affordable capital. Those that have been affected the most are

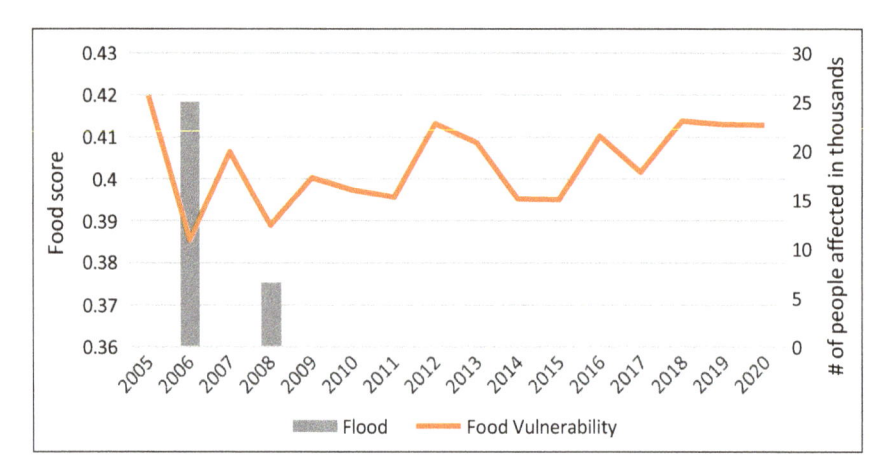

Figure 4.36. Food security vulnerability to climate change impacts (index) and the effect of climate-related events, 2005–2020.

Note: Food vulnerability refers to food security vulnerability to climate change. The axis captures the food security vulnerability index to climate change, while the right shows the number of people affected by climate-related events.
Source: ND-GAIN Data and World Bank Data.

small-scale farmers. According to FAO *et al.* (2023), approximately 35.8% of the population was affected by moderate or severe food insecurity between 2019 and 2021.

4.13.3. *Food import dependency*

The COVID-19 pandemic has exposed inherent vulnerabilities of Suriname's food security architecture, as evidenced by the negative impacts the pandemic has had on the country's overall food production system (GCF, 2020). Additionally, the surge in global inflation has negatively affected the country's food import bill.

According to the World Bank, food imports as a share of total merchandise imports have seen a slight increase in 2021 relative to the previous year. However, while this may be the case, the country's share of food imports is still lower than the Caribbean average. Interestingly, the share of food production in GDP has been on the increase since 2015, moving from about 5–8% by 2020.

Country Briefs 73

Suriname's food imports as a share of total merchandise imports exhibited a fluctuating pattern during the period 2005–2021 (Figure 4.37). The ratio trended upward from a period-low of 9.5% in 2005 to 15.2% by 2010 and then fluctuated thereafter until reaching a peak of 18.9% in 2016. The ratio then declined continuously, reaching 13.1% in 2019, after which it underwent a final turnaround, rebounding to 16.1% in 2021. Meanwhile, food production as a share of nominal GDP displayed two distinct patterns. The ratio fluctuated between 6.3% and a period-low of 4.7% over the period 2005–2015 and then steadily increased to reach a period-high of 8.1% in 2020.

4.13.4. *Agricultural investment by the private sector and public debt*

The share of domestic credit allocated to agriculture in Suriname displayed a downward trend since 2007 (Figure 4.38). Specifically, the ratio declined from a period-high of around 4.6% in 2007 to less than 2.4% in

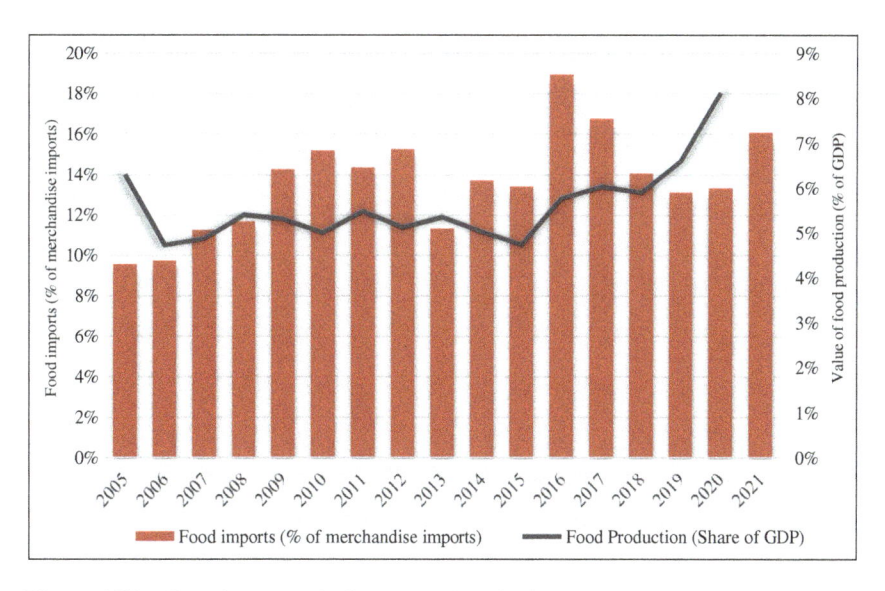

Figure 4.37. Food imports (% of total merchandise imports) and value of food production (% of GDP), 2005–2021.

Source: World Bank Data and FAOSTAT.

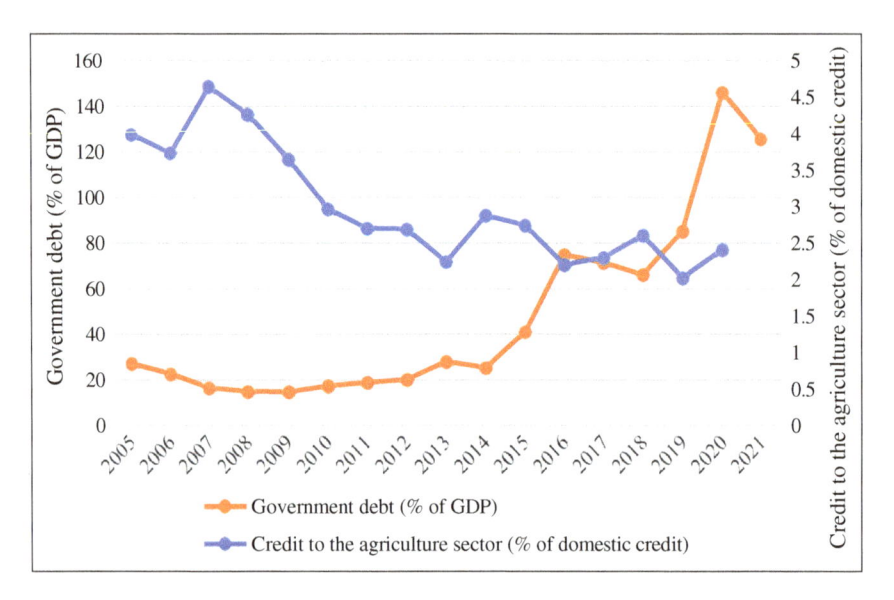

Figure 4.38. Credit to the agriculture sector (as a share of total domestic credit) and government debt, 2005–2021.

Source: FAOSTAT and IMF Data.

2020. This pattern seems to confirm the difficulty in accessing affordable capital for farmers and even raises doubts about the country's food security outlook. In essence, less than 3 cents of every dollar of domestic credit was allocated to the agriculture sector in 2020.

Notably, Suriname's debt burden has increased sharply over the review period. The evolution of Suriname's debt burden, as shown in Figure 4.38, is characterized by two contrasting sub-periods. During the first phase, from 2005 to 2014, the ratio displayed relative stability but then increased appreciably thereafter from 25% in 2014 to a period-high of 146.1% in 2020. While the ratio declined marginally in 2021, it remained precariously high. While this most recent decline is commendable, it must be noted that the 2021 ratio is significantly above the recommended sustainable threshold of 64% for emerging economies (Caner *et al.*, 2010).

4.14. Trinidad and Tobago

Table 4.14. Selected macroeconomic indicators: Trinidad and Tobago.

Population (total)	1,525,663 (2021)
Rural population (% of total pop)	47 (2021)
GDP, PPP (current international $)	38,612,227.87 (2021)
GDP per capita, PPP (international $)	25,308.5 (2021)
Income level (by per capita GNI)	High Income
HDI	0.81 (2021) 56 out of 191 (2020)
Level of development	Developing
Debt-to-GDP ratio	0.16 (2007)
Ease of doing business rank	61.3 (105 out of 190) (2020)
Moderate of severe insecurity (%)	43.3 (2019–2021)
Global competitiveness index	58.3 (78 out of 141) (2019)
Agriculture as a share of GDP	1.0% (2021)
Employment in agriculture (% of Total employment)	2.9% (2020)
Inflation, consumer prices (annual %)	2.1% (2021)
Total land area	5.1 (sq. km thousands)
Arable land %	4.8% (2020)
Total agricultural area	10.5% (2020)
Crop production index	103.3 (2020)
Livestock production index	104.7 (2020)
Cereal production	5,734 (2020)

Source: World Bank Data, FAOSTAT.

4.14.1. *Overview of the agricultural sector*

The agriculture sector in Trinidad and Tobago, though relatively small compared to the other sectors (less than 2%), is regarded as socially important, especially for those living in rural areas. Locally produced agricultural food products are usually sold locally to markets, hotels, and restaurants (Caribbean Agribusiness, 2022c).

Primary agricultural export commodities include sugar, cocoa, and coffee, while others include coconut, rice, citrus fruits, vegetables, and poultry (Crop Trust, 2023). Based on the latest census data on agriculture in Trinidad and Tobago, there were around 18,951 farmers in the country, occupying almost 84,990 hectares of land, of which more than half were privately owned (Central Statistical Office, 2022).

4.14.2. *Impact of climate change on food production*

Some of the main constraints affecting domestic agricultural production in Trinidad and Tobago are the availability of agricultural land and climate-related events, such as flooding, landslide, and drought. Notably, the country relies heavily on food imports, with the United States satisfying around 40% of its total food demand. However, the global increases in commodity prices and climate-related events are likely to impact agricultural exports adversely (ITA, 2022).

The food score of Trinidad and Tobago fluctuated significantly between 2005 and 2015, initially increasing to a peak of 0.45 in 2009 and then declining to a period-low of 0.39 from 2012 to 2014. After climbing to a score of 0.40 in 2015, it has since remained constant (Figure 4.39). The most recent score signifies a stabilisation of the country's risk exposure with respect to climate-related events, with Trinidad and Tobago ranking 66 out of 189 countries on the ND-GAIN food vulnerability index.

4.14.3. *Food import dependency*

Food production as a share of GDP fluctuated between 2005 and 2020 but remained below one during the entire period. Food imports as a share of

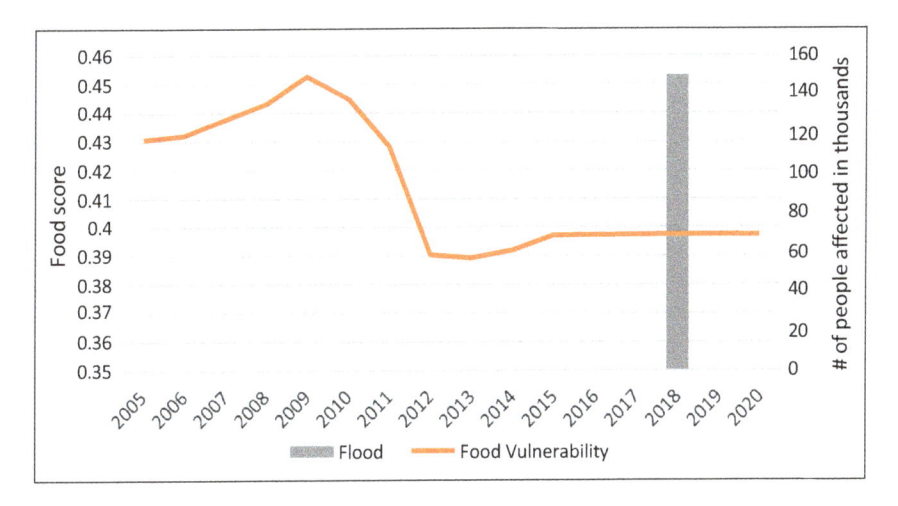

Figure 4.39. Food security vulnerability to climate change impacts (index) and the effect of climate-related events, 2005–2020.

Note: Food vulnerability refers to food security vulnerability to climate change. The axis captures the food security vulnerability index to climate change, while the right shows the number of people affected by climate-related events.
Source: ND-GAIN Data and World Bank Data.

merchandise imports also fluctuated during the corresponding period but exhibited a general upward trend since 2013, peaking at 19% in 2020 and then tapering off marginally to approximately 18% in 2021 (Figure 4.40).

A possible consequence of Trinidad and Tobago's relatively low food production is its high food dependency, with the country relying on imports for about 85% of its food supply. Over the past few years, the country's economy has been declining due to the slowdown of its petroleum sector. Additionally, agriculture production has remained volatile due to the frequency of climate related events. Food security in the country remains a challenge, given the global and domestic increase in food prices coupled with the decline in income (IDB, 2018).

The production of sugar, previously one of the country's main agricultural exports, came almost to an almost immediate halt in 2007 due to the loss of the EU's preferential market, with production ceasing altogether shortly thereafter. Similarly, coconut production has also been on the decline since the 1990s, as well as coffee and cocoa production. The latter

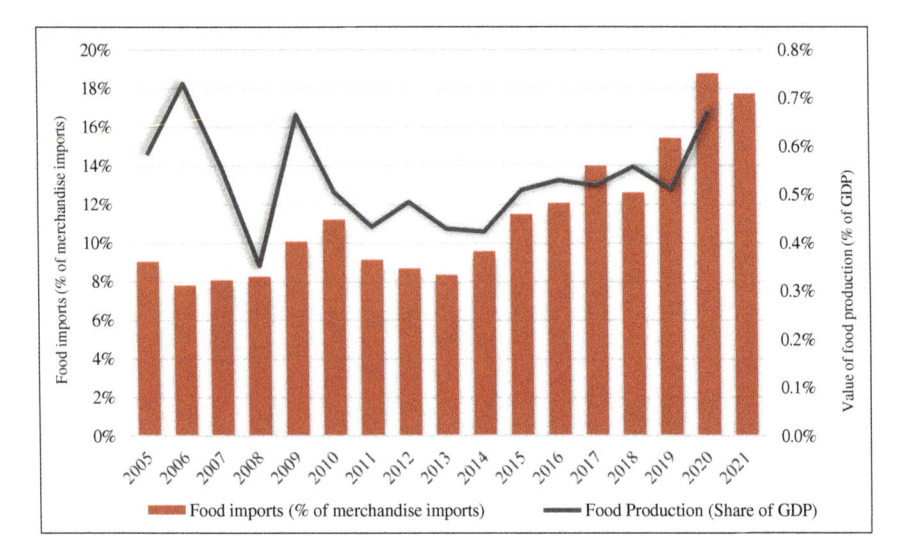

78 *Achieving Global Food Security: The Caribbean Experience and Beyond*

Figure 4.40. Food imports (% of total merchandise imports) and value of food production (% of GDP), 2005–2021.

Note: Food imports represent food imports (% of total merchandise trade).
Source: World Bank Data and FAOSTAT.

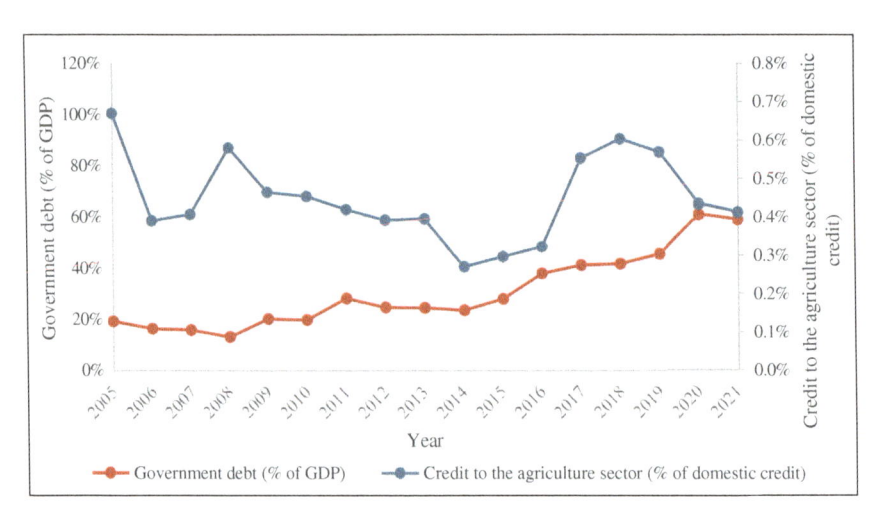

Figure 4.41. Credit to the agriculture sector (as a share of total domestic credit) and government debt, 2005–2021.

Source: FAOSTAT and IMF Data.

two commodities have been plagued with pests and diseases. Rice has also seen a major decline in production since the 1990s due to low productivity. However, production of other crops, such as tomatoes, hot petters, and root crops, has increased in recent years (Shik *et al.*, 2018).

4.14.4. *Investment in agriculture and public debt*

Similar to food production, the share of domestic credit allocated to agriculture fluctuated but remained below 1% during the review period (Figure 4.41). This implies that less than 1 cent of every dollar of domestic credit goes to the agriculture sector. Meanwhile, as shown in Figure 4.41, Trinidad and Tobago's debt-to-GDP ratio increased steadily from 2005 to 2021, moving from around 19% in 2005 to a period-high of 61% in 2020 and then contracting slightly to 59% in 2021.

Chapter 5

Strategic Policy Recommendations

Given the current global food security predicament and the devastating impact of the COVID-19 pandemic that continues to rattle economies, especially those of the developing world, in the future, governments must consider the most cost-effective and efficient solutions. Moreover, improving economic access to food will require a pragmatic and innovative approach. This final chapter outlines strategic policy recommendations to guide the region in prioritising efforts that will lead to greater food security and hence achieve its vision 25 by 2025. The latter speaks to the imbalances between food consumption and food production in the Caribbean. The aim is to reduce the region's food importation bill by 25% by 2025. As pointed out elsewhere, globally, the world is faced with food shortages coupled with high prices of imported food, fertilisers, and other agricultural inputs. The current transportation and logistics crisis is heightening these challenges. In the Caribbean Region, member states have been largely affected by these developments through higher prices of food. Most commodities imported include wheat, animal feed mostly made up of corn and soya, and a range of processed foods.

Importantly, Vision 25 by 2025 seeks to enhance food security in the region through a series of strategic actions and recommendations geared at overcoming hurdles in transportation and logistics, technology transfer, trade barriers, and even getting young people to be part of the food production system. In absolute terms, the 25% reduction in food import bills is around US$6 billion. To date, several key stakeholders, including the private sector and commercial and financial institutions, have expressed

President Ali and other regional leaders at Opening Ceremony of Agriculture Investment Forum and Expo, Guyana 2022. (Office of the President Photo)

their unwavering support. The plan to reduce food importation by 25% by 2025 is driven by a Special Ministerial Taskforce on Food Production & Food Security and the CARCIOM private sector organisation supported by the CARCIOM Secretariat.

For the Caribbean Region to reduce its food importation bill by 25% in 2025, its 2021 food importation bill will have to be reduced by approximately US$2.7 billion (Figure 5.1). Therefore, there is an urgent need for the region to take purposeful and immediate actions to curb its dependence on food importation. Some of the steps the region may pursue to achieve Vision 25 by 2025 are described in the following section.

5.1. Establishment of a Regional Agro-Tech Campus

The Regional Agro-Tech Campus (RATC) will promote translational research and experimental development of agriculture, technology, and innovation to address the current food insecurity challenges of the region. Particularly, the RATC will focus on developing entrepreneurship,

Strategic Policy Recommendations 83

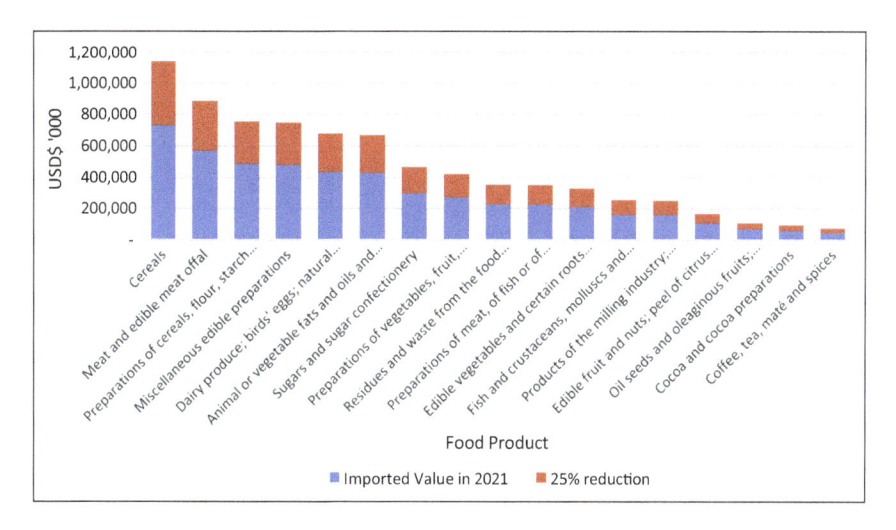

Figure 5.1. Food imports as per category for the entire region.
Source: UN Comtrade Database.

specifically start-ups, in the life science field while supporting advanced and specialised training of researchers, and other technicians, in the areas of agricultural and environmental biotechnology and food and nutrition. The approach is to revolutionize the Caribbean food and agriculture industry while strengthening food security in the region and becoming the region's leading institute of technology for food and environmental science (Figure 5.2).

At its core, the RATC will have several key incubation facilities targeting small- and medium-sized enterprises (SMEs) and start-ups in various life science areas. To facilitate this process, start-ups will be provided access to critical infrastructure and facilities, mentoring, and even networking platforms during their early stages of development. The aim is to help start-ups survive the initial period of their existence by providing specialised support services. Start-up companies will be incubated following a selection process by a technical selection committee. The core functions of the RATC will include the following:

a. **Branding/Marketing Support:** Greater focus will be placed on developing and supporting a product launch platform and testing. This will require the RATC to collaborate with public institutions providing

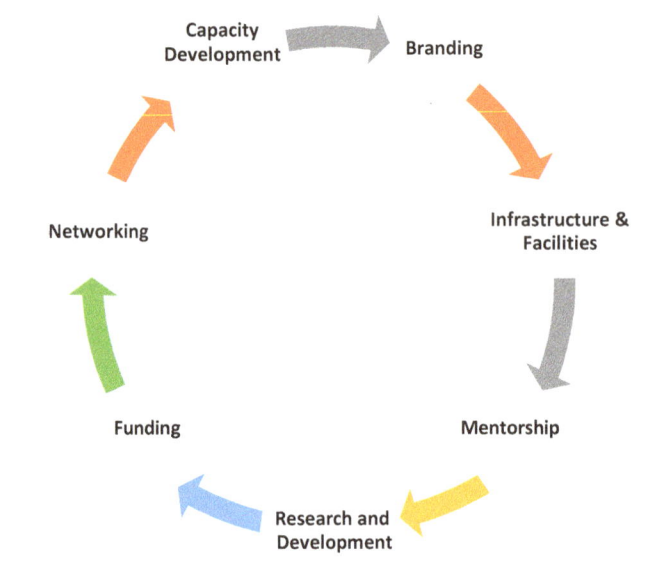

84 *Achieving Global Food Security: The Caribbean Experience and Beyond*

Figure 5.2. Key functions of the Regional Agro-Tech Campus.

Center, Barbados Prime Minister Mia Mottley, at Argi Investment Forum and Expo, May 2022.

extension services to farmers and the private sector. The latter is to facilitate the deployment of developed technologies to industries and other agricultural players, allowing farmers and producers' organisations to discover the various high-tech services offered by the RATC and stimulate growth in the agri start-up ecosystem. Furthermore, as part of the awareness campaign, the RATC will collaborate with key partners, academic institutions, start-ups, and individuals.

b. **Technical/Scientific Expertise:** These experts will offer support and mentorship to the incubates/start-ups.

c. **Mentoring Support:** Support will be provided at all levels, including in-house by the RATC scientific/technical team and through specialised workshops. To enhance the efficiency of this programme, a more structured and targeted approach will also be taken that consists of one-on-one mentoring.

Officials from CARICOM, Guyana's Ministry of Agriculture, with past and current students at Guyana School of Agriculture Shade House Project site, Mon Repos, Guyana.

Location: National Agricultural Research & Extension Institute (NAREI), Mon Repos, Guyana.

d. **Research and Development:** This will play an integral part in expanding the knowledge barrier, developing new technologies and finding innovative solutions to complex problems.

86 *Achieving Global Food Security: The Caribbean Experience and Beyond*

e. **Funding:** Financial support will be provided to start-ups through the incubators to assist with prototype development, trials of products, launching, and commercialisation. This is crucial, especially given the financial challenges technology-driven start-ups tend to face during their initial phases of development. This assistance will help to develop meritorious ideas, innovations, and technologies to a sustainable level where they can eventually raise capital from financial institutions independently. As discussed later, this process could be facilitated through a thriving ecosystem.
f. **Networking:** Incubation facilities will benefit from collaboration with national, regional, and global organisations, including academic institutions. Networking will also be facilitated through the innovative ecosystem (Figure 5.3), where start-ups will be exposed to not only

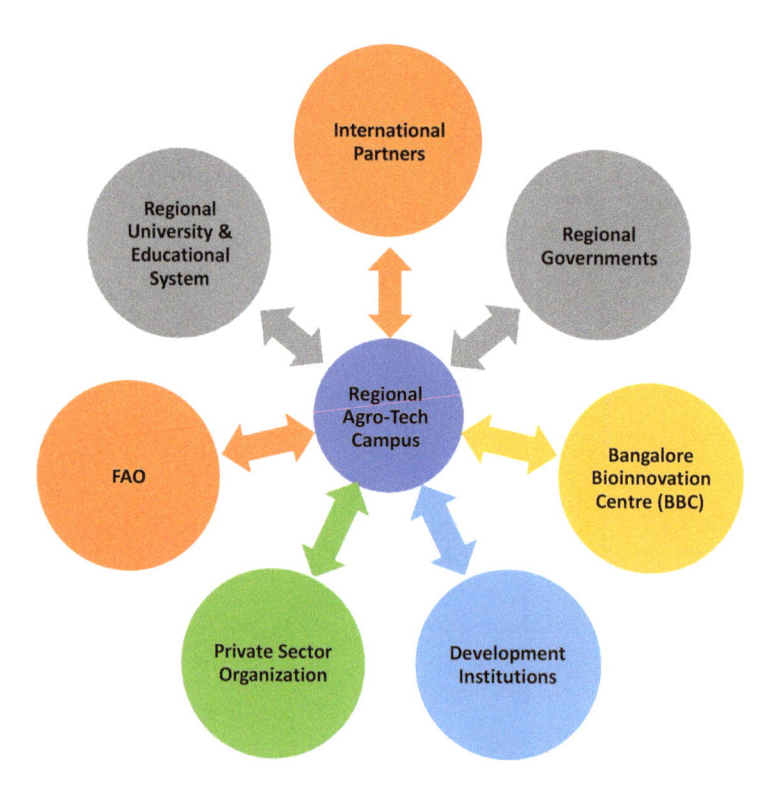

Figure 5.3. The innovative ecosystem.

educational institutions but also the private sector and financial institutions.
g. **Capacity Building:** The focus will be on developing training programmes to support start-ups, expand R&D in broad areas of life science and technologies, and enhance the quality of education and research at partnering academic institutions.

The RATC will also promote the development of a regional brand of technologies and products developed by the centre. To stimulate growth, development, and supprt, a percentage of the proceeds from selling these products will be assigned to a special fund to help alleviate hunger.

To achieve the overall objective of the RATC, there will be a great need for harmonisation among major stakeholders and development partners (Figure 5.3), ultimately creating a robust and innovative ecosystem. Major research institutes, technical centres, international partners, regional governments, the Food and Agriculture Organization of the United Nations (FAO), the Bangalore Bioinnovation Centre (BBC), development institutions as well as the regional private sector bodies will have an integral role in the Regional Agro-Tech Campus to ensure the proliferation of a sustainable and innovative ecosystem. Their respective roles may be as follows:

I. **International Partners:** Leveraging strategic relationships and close ties with key international partners is critical to help foster innovation across the ecosystem and benefit from proven toolkits and frameworks created through evidence-based experience (WEF, 2022c).
II. **Regional Governments:** To strengthen the Caribbean's agriculture and food processing capacity and hence improve the region's access to food security, not only do we need technological interventions, but also from a government-to-government perspective, nurturing and strengthening partnerships will become critical. This component is also critical to leverage experienced human capacities in the broad areas of life science that exist outside the region.
III. **Bangalore Bio Innovation Centre (BBC):** The BBC is a consortium between the Government of India and other key local

President Ali and First Lady Arya Ali with Caribbean Leaders at the Opening Ceremony of the Agri Investment Froum and Expo, May, 2022.

institutions, including the Department of Biotechnology, Department of Electronics, IT, BT, and S&T. In essence, the BBC is a state-of-the-art transnational centre that focuses on research and entrepreneurship to address the needs of start-ups in life science including Healthcare (MedTech and Biopharma), Agriculture, Food and Nutrition. Having the BBC as part of the ecosystem will allow the RATC to leverage much-needed capacity and expertise from a prolific sister institution like the BBC.

IV. **Development Institutions:** Establishing relationships with (and fortifying existing) key development institutions, particularly financials, is critical to address potential challenges start-ups face in accessing institutional credit primarily because of low capital, absence of credit history, and lack of collateral. From the RATC perspective, working in tandem with key development institutions will allow for a holistic approach in tackling key regional challenges such as food insecurity, hunger, pest infestation, and low yield, while at the same time working towards global development goals such as the SDGs.

V. **Regional Private Sector Organisations:** It is well established that education is a private good. However, for it to become a true public good, both the government and private sector must work together (Aneja and Lalvani, 2021). This proposed public private partnership (PPP) is crucial to boost regional food production capacity and address the ubiquitous shortcomings of sustainability, efficiency, and inclusivity. Under the PPP model, the role of the private sector will focus on developing agile business models while creating the necessary platforms or distribution channels to help deploy the technologies.

VI. **Food and Agriculture Organization of the United Nations (FAO):** The FAO is a specialised agency that focuses on ending hunger. One of its key goals is to achieve food security for all and ensure that everyone has access to high-quality food to live healthy lives. The FAO works in over 130 countries worldwide and has a membership of 194 countries. The FAO "believes that Science, Technology and Innovation (STI) can accelerate the transformation of agri-food systems so that they become MORE efficient, inclusive, resilient, and sustainable agri-food systems for better production, better nutrition, a better environment, and a better life, leaving no one behind" (FAO, 2023).

VII. **Regional Universities and Educational System:** This element is critical to address the research and development needs to foster a sustainable biological and synthetic system focusing on food and the environment. The aim is to explore biological resources to address key challenges affecting the region in agriculture while ensuring the protection of our environment and promoting innovation for the bioeconomy. This organisation will allow the RATC to leverage much of its expertise and facilitate crucial knowledge transfer and innovation.

5.2. Roraima as an Alternative Food Supplier

The State of Roraima is bordered on the north by Venezuela, east by Guyana, and outh by the state of the Amazonas. Roraima has a population of around 514,229 inhabitants and a gross domestic product of around US$2.1 billion (2016 data) (ABDIB, 2020). The state boasts a land area of 223,645 km sq., a human development index of 0.756, and a total road network of 8,323 km (*ibid*).

90 *Achieving Global Food Security: The Caribbean Experience and Beyond*

Guyana has over 18 million hectares of pristine, tropical rain forest.

The state of Roraima is seen as a strategic trading partner given its ideal location, with proximity to the Caribbean. As a major trading partner, Roraima would undoubtedly help address and circumvent the omnipresent challenges of logistical and supply chain disruption, hence, improving food security in the region.

In 2021, Roraima exported US$330 million, making the state 22nd out of 27 exporters in Brazil (OEC, 2023). In 2021, Roraima export basket comprised "Soya beans: other than seed (US$71.4 million), Sausages, similar products of meat (US$45.4 million), Margarine, except liquid margarine (US$44.8 million), Refined soya-bean oil, not chemically modified (US$30 million), and Refined sugar, in solid form, nes, pure sucrose (US$22.7 million)" (*ibid*).[1]

Based on Table 5.1, the Caribbean Region has imported around US$1.8 billion in food supplies from 10 of its top trading partners outside of the region in 2021 (column 2). Of this amount, the USA satisfied at

---
[1] The classification of these commodities is based on the Harmonised System (HS) Codes 1992 for six digits. For the purpose of comparison, these commodities are considered "Roraima Specific Food Commodities".

least 66% of the region's food supply demand, followed by the Netherlands (7%) and Canada (7.15%). Notably, during the same period, the Caribbean imported around US$191 million of the total food import bill in food supplies similar to those exported by Roraima (column 3). This amount represents a total of 10% of the region's total food import bill. This analysis speaks to the fact that Roraima could, at the minimum, supply the Caribbean with at least 10% of its food supply needs, holding everything else equal. Figure 5.4 captures the above pattern.

There are several advantages to this approach. Firstly, the strategic location of Roraima makes it an ideal location for trade with the Caribbean. The proximity of the State of Roraima to the Caribbean will significantly reduce logistical burdens that are ubiquitous with long-distance shipping and handling. Secondly, Guyana, with its vast resources,

Table 5.1. The Caribbean top 10 trading partners.

Year	Top 10 trading partners[2] (1)	Total food import bill (US$)[3] (2)	Total import food bill (Roraima specific food commodities in US$)[4] (3)	% of Roraima specific food commodities imported[5] (4)
2021	Argentina	24,829,112	18,411,546	74%
2021	Canada	135,703,356	3,329,082	2%
2021	Colombia	40,379,362	22,594,324	56%
2021	Germany	26,951,425	1,436,673	5%
2021	Guatemala	69,221,332	44,389,420	64%
2021	Indonesia	10,468,327	2,059,347	20%
2021	Mexico	91,882,800	7,409,792	8%
2021	Netherlands	144,295,203	10,426,845	7%
2021	United Kingdom	74,097,079	4,875,008	7%
2021	USA	1,268,480,060	76,364,410	6%
Total		1,886,308,056	191,296,447	10%

Source: Authors' own calculation using data from the UN Comtrade Database.

---

[2] Top 10 food trading partners with the Caribbean Region.
[3] Total cost of food imports into the Caribbean in nominal USD.
[4] Total cost of food imports similar to those commodities produced in Roraima.
[5] Percentage of food imports similar to those exported by Roraima.

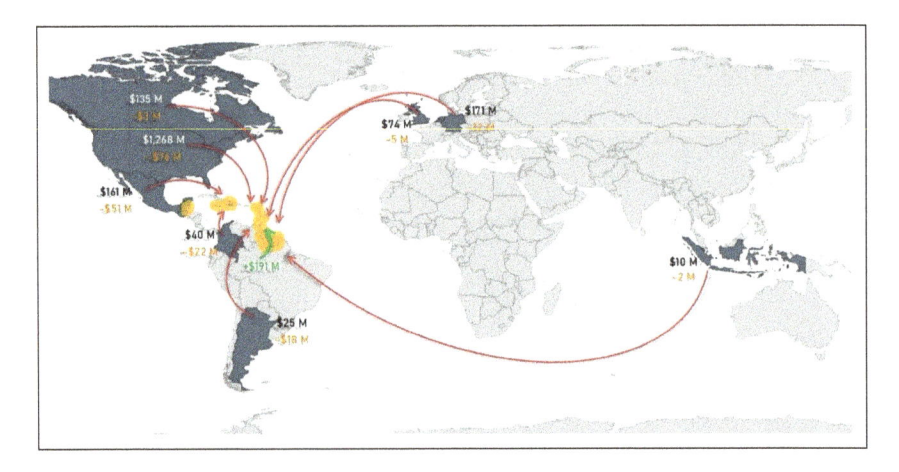

Figure 5.4. The Caribbean and its top 10 trading partners.

Note: The red arrows identify the Caribbean's top 10 trading partners in 2021, the estimated value of total food imports (positive figures), and the estimated value of the Roraima-specific food export commodities (negative figures).

could become the regional trade, transportation, and logistics hub between Roraima and by extension South America and the Caribbean.

5.3. Commercialisation of Food Supply

To ensure that food production within the region is sustained at a level that meets the region's food consumption needs while creating new opportunities for the enhancement or creation of export markets, support must be channelled to the transitioning of small-scale agricultural systems into more competitive and commercially dynamic ones.

The most notable policy interventions and actions with the potential to achieve the greatest return and create the necessary enabling environment to foster the commercialization of food supply are described in the following sections.

5.3.1. *E-Agriculture*

E-Agriculture targets the enhancement of rural and agricultural development through the application of innovative information and communication technologies (ICT). For CARICOM, the emphasis should involve the following:

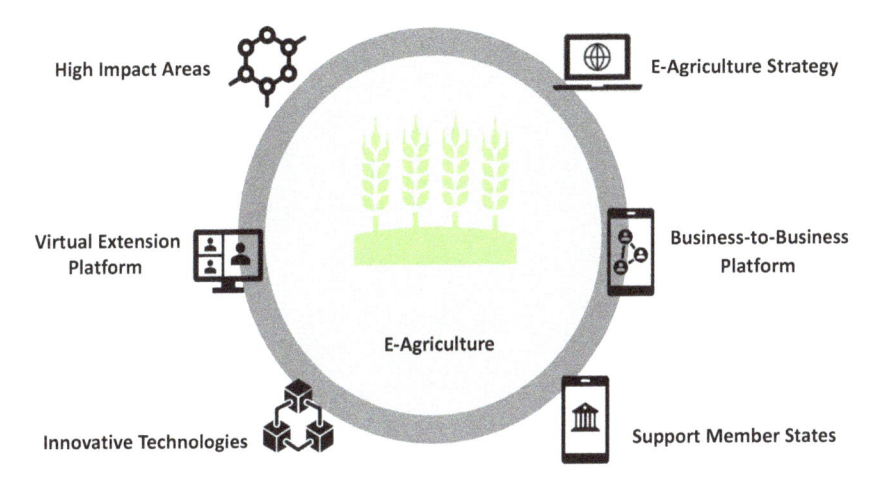

Figure 5.5. Caribbean E-Agriculture model.

1. **Development of a regional e-agriculture strategy:** This will help promote an incentive regime to encourage greater technology adoption.
2. **Development and implementation of a business-to-business (B2B) Platform:** This will facilitate efficient interactions among private sector buyers and sellers of agricultural products and produce nationally and across the region.
3. **Deployment of a government-to-government (G2G) portal:** This is aimed at providing focused and direct engagement between member states through the various CARICOM Ministers of Agriculture to foster greater intra-regional trade of agricultural produce and commodities.
4. **Support to member states:** This can be achieved by engaging, identifying, and packaging innovative technologies in ICT (drones and other precision agriculture techniques) for application in appropriate sectors in the region.
5. **Development of a virtual extension platform:** This will support the provision of regional extension services and access to key subject matter specialists.
6. **Identification of high-impact areas for farmer exposure (climate-smart agriculture remains relevant):** This will minimize the potential loss caused by climate-related events.

5.4. Caricom Cross Border Agri-Food Investment Strategy

One notable policy intervention with the potential to create the necessary enabling environment to foster the commercialization of food supply in the Caribbean Region is the development of a CARICOM Cross-Border Agri-Food Investment Strategy to support production corridors.

President Ali at Santa Fe Farm, North Rupununi, Guyana. To his left in red shirt is Minister of Agriculture, Hon. Zulfikar Mustapha.

Cross-border agricultural investments have proven to be effective in promoting technology transfer, capacity building and development, including skills training. These developments can lead to increased agricultural productivity, food security, and access to capital.

The CARICOM Agri-Food System Agenda identified the **development of production zones** in larger land mass territories for Member States to facilitate cross-border investment as an immediate policy solution to be implemented in the region as investment production is promoted. This requires the following:

1. updating land-use policies in the respective member states;
2. mapping of production activities in the region;

3. addressing taxation, trading, and quota policies;
4. reducing regulatory and administrative border procedures.

The Cross-Border Agri-Food Investment Strategy will facilitate intra-regional agri-food trade across the entire food value chain while focusing on areas such as the following:

1. **Scale and sourcing factors:** To become more competitive domestically, regionally and internationally, the sector must improve its efficiency. Therefore, a priority is to develop a scale to ensure that supply meets demand is a priority. An analysis of the comparative advantages of the production capacity of the region should also be conducted to guide investment.
2. **Port capacity and access:** Cost-effective and reliable connections are important for the efficient movement of commodities. In this regard, transportation infrastructure in the region, seaports, and airports must be developed to facilitate intra-regional exports.
3. **Cross-border Cooperation:** To ensure that the regional markets have access to nutritious food, cross-border cooperation is necessary at the government and private sector levels.
4. **Cross-border Regional brands:** Opportunities also exist through cross-border integration for regional brands to develop and for food tourism to grow regionally.

Specifically, there may be a need for added focus on the following strategies:

5.4.1. *Removal of non-tariff barriers to trade*

The Revised Treaty of Chaguaramas provides for unrestricted movement of trade originating within the region and recognizes the right of member states to impose legitimate technical requirements on imports. It outlaws all quantitative restrictions, including import licensing and administrative measures restricting intra-regional trade.

The Common External Tariff (CET) regime, the major instrument for providing regional producers with the level of protection needed to support production and facilitate intra-regional trade, recognised in its original design that agricultural products required higher levels of protection

96 *Achieving Global Food Security: The Caribbean Experience and Beyond*

than those accorded to most non-agricultural products. While some of those concerns may persist, it should be noted that many of those products have been prioritised at the regional level for special attention. These include sheep and poultry, eggs, pork, goat meat, several dried and salted fish products, onions and shallots, maize, and refined sugar.

Ariel view of Muneshwer's Wharf, Water Street, Georgetown, Guyana.

5.4.2. *De-risking of the agricultural sector*

Fresh produce is integral to food security.    Fresh produce from a farm in Guyana.

CARICOM member states, through a very deliberate policy instrument, must make the sector more attractive to the private sector and other potential investors. This intervention is critical for strengthening the financial architecture surrounding agriculture/agri-business in the CARICOM region. It also requires creative and innovative approaches to financial literacy and financing of the regional agricultural sector. Specifically, the following policy actions are being proposed:

1. Creation of an Agricultural Catastrophe Fund at the national level with linkages to the regional Caribbean Catastrophe Risk Insurance Facility (CCRIF), which would allow for the development of a stable and robust agriculture sector;
2. Enactment of a Regional/National Food Security Procurement Policy that promote an agreed percentage of all foods destined for government institutions (prisons, hospitals, and schools) to be sourced locally/regionally;
3. Adoption of a Regional Incentive System for potential investors in the sector;
4. Adoption of alternative financing systems that require less sovereign support, such as the stock market and crowd-funding mechanism;
5. Creation of regional investment systems that allows for greater predictability of the sector by financing institutions;
6. Completion of the framework for the free movement of skilled agricultural workers and subject matter specialists across the region.

5.4.3. *Improving transportation and logistics regionally*

The key steps required for improving transportation and logistics regionally include the following:

1. Development and agreement on a special incentive regime and system for transporting regional agricultural produce and products;
2. Creation of regional trade, transportation, and logistics hubs or corridors to foster greater intra-regional trade, including a Northern Caribbean Trade Corridor, an Eastern Caribbean Trade Corridor, and a Southern Caribbean Trade Corridor.

5.4.4. *Removal of technical barriers*

The following steps are needed for the removal of technical barriers:

1. Strengthening the role of the Caribbean Agricultural Health and Food Safety Agency (CAHFSA), including its ability to act as an arbiter in SPS-related disputes;
2. Creation and immediate implementation of a Regional Trade and Information portal for member states and the private sector, which would allow for the efficient distribution of food supplies and the identification of opportunities throughout the region;
3. Establishment of CARICOM Agricultural Non-Tariff Barriers Online complaints mechanism and identification of the respective national focal points for information sharing;
4. Adoption and implementation of Sanitary and Phytosanitary (SPS) Dispute Resolution Mechanisms for the CARICOM region;
5. Adoption of the Regional Policy on Agricultural Health and Food Safety;
6. Implementation of the Fisheries SPS protocols for the region;
7. Adoption and implementation, by all member states, of the soon-to-be-completed harmonised sanitary and phytosanitary (SPS) measures and protocols for 19 specially selected agricultural commodities to facilitate intra-regional agri-food trade and to support food security of member states;
8. Adoption and implementation over the next three years of the Regional Policy on Trade in Animals and Animal Products;
9. Creation of a Regional Food Imports/Production Monitoring Mechanism to provide real-time information on the potential for regional production and supply of key food items and inputs;
10. Adoption and utilisation of electronic processing systems for all SPS-related permits by all member states;
11. Acceleration of the Trade Facilitation Reform process for CARICOM to improve the ease of doing business with a focus on digitalization.

5.4.5. *Investment in production, research and development*

Following are the key steps that focus on investment in production, research and development:

1. creation of an information and statistical system underpinned by the Regional Strategy for the Development of Statistics (RSDS) to support evidence-based decision-making;

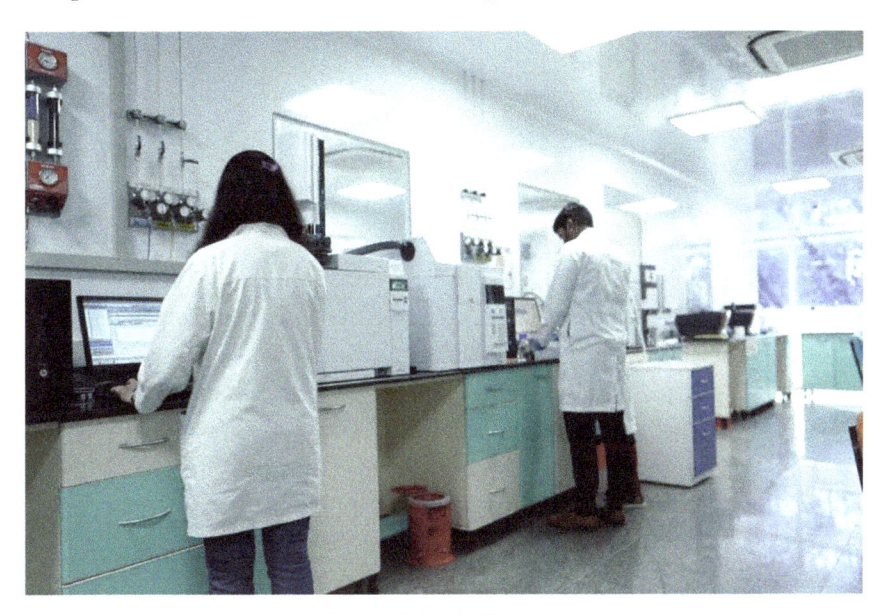

Research lab in Guyana.

2. development of a private sector-led regional training and accreditation programme to improve the number of agricultural subject matter specialists throughout the CARICOM region to address the expected growth in the sector;
3. implementation of capacity building for the ministries with responsibilities for Agriculture and Fisheries to be more responsive to the needs of the sector;
4. development of production zones in larger land mass territories for member states to facilitate cross-border investment;

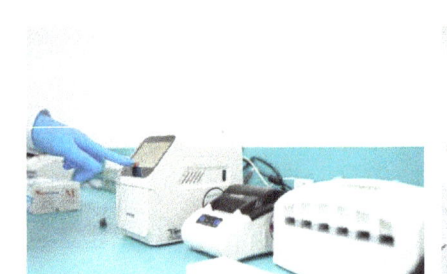

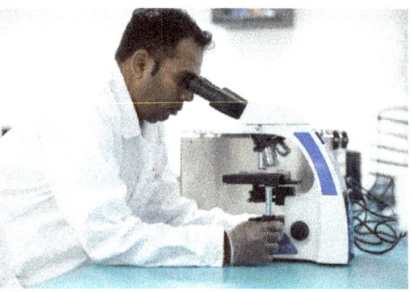

Research lab in Guyana.

5. re-engineering of the regional production systems through the digitization of the agri-business sector;
6. development of the agriculture value chain using scientific and technological innovations;
7. expansion of agricultural production and promote the availability of inputs: Led by the Caribbean Agricultural Research and Development Institute (CARDI), the programme will establish strategic supply locations in the member states, which will be able to supply the region with high-quality planting material. Framework for contract farming and other mechanisms to promote efficient transmission of market and price information throughout the supply chain.

Chapter 6

Works in the Pipeline and Way Forward: Guyana

6.1. Corn and Soya Bean Pilot Project

Guyana aims to become self-sufficient in corn and soya beans for its poultry industry, which currently imports over US$25 million for proteins, even as it increases its capacity to export to CARICOM. Annually, the CARICOM Market for corn and soya beans is US$137.9 million. Success in implementing this project will position Guyana to tap into this lucrative market.

In 2021, a consortium of local investors successfully cultivated 115 acres of soya bean and 5 acres of corn. With almost a GY$1.2 billion investment by the government, the pilot project made significant progress. For instance, in 2022, 40 km of the access road was completed, and 463 tonnes of soya beans were harvested. Furthermore, work has commenced on constructing the silos/storage facilities to process and store corn and soya beans. In 2023, a wharf for corn and soybean at Tacama will be added to aid in transporting the commodity to market.

Moreover, the consortium plans to increase acres under cultivation to 9,000 by the end of 2023, 26,000 acres is projected to be under cultivation for 2024 and 36,000 acres for 2025.

Ongoing works on one of the silos.

6.2. Bilateral Partnership to Advance Agriculture

Some important bilateral partnerships aimed at the advancement of agriculture are as follows:

a. Guyana–Barbados: The Saint Barnabas Accord signed between Barbados and Guyana allowed the two countries to strengthen existing ties and collaboration among several sectors, mainly agriculture, aquaculture, and food security: extractive sector, transportation, trade and business development, manufacturing, energy, and even social services such as education.

As it relates to agriculture, Guyana will supply Barbados with several agricultural products (beef, corn, soya, fruits, vegetables, and even poultry and livestock products) while allocating a share of its land to Barbados for the purpose of farming and livestock rearing at a concessional rate. Other initiatives include supporting Barbados in becoming the centre of meat and fish processing products. On the receiving side, Guyana will be benefitting from the supply of black belly sheep from Barbados, among others. In both countries, food terminal facilities will also be established to facilitate export to other countries, while efforts will be made to establish an exchange programme to facilitate aquaculture training.

Guyana's President Irfaan Ali and Barbados Prime Minister Mia Mottley inspect Guyanese made products at the Umana Yana, Georgetown, Guyana.

Already, the two countries have made progress in the following areas:

1. Initiating and setting up of Barbados–Guyana food terminal in Barbados;
2. Establishing a trade committee to address barriers to trade (including SPS matters);
3. Setting up a Barbados Brown's Pond Prawns Project, with projected revenue of US$2.4 million;
4. Distributing 500 Black Giant to Barbados to boost poultry production efforts;

5. Providing Tilapia Technical support to commence aquaculture production at Brown's Reservoir;
6. Providing technical support to develop shade house technology to start the process of climate-smart agriculture.

Plans are also in place to promote the cultivation of millet in Barbados. Besides the nutritional value of millet, the product is suitable for diabetics and could serve as a replacement for high-carb grains such as rice.

b. Guyana–Trinidad and Tobago signed an MOU to renew and enhance cooperation on May 22, 2022, on agriculture and food security, security, energy, infrastructure, trade, and investment. A joint technical working group has already been functional with other areas of support for coconut and shade houses.

c. Guyana and Antigua and Barbuda signed an MOU on Economic Cooperation on May 20, 2022. Other countries with enhanced bilateral include Suriname and St Vincent and the Grenadines.

6.3. Building a Regional Food Hub

As part of its Vision 25 by 2025 plan, significant budgetary allocations have already been made towards the diversification of agricultural production, the creation of a robust marketing system, and the strengthening of a resilient and sustainable agri-food system.

Guyana's strategic location on the coast of South America allows access to both the Caribbean and South American markets. Guyana is set to be a major commercial centre as the economy is transformed to advance agriculture and establish a manufacturing base. Therefore, in 2023, the government will invest heavily in a food hub.

This food hub will aid in aggregating food products for distribution, storing semi-processed and processed products for transport to the markets, and marketing by matching buyers and sellers.

The investment in 2023 will be in a state-of-the-art central packaging facility equipped with receiving, cleaning, temperature-controlled storage, and processing facilities. This would further need to be supported by an efficient transportation fleet of the appropriate type.

This food hub is aligned with the regional Barbados-based Logistics Hubs. These hubs will enhance regional logistics and supply chains, boost intraregional trade, and ensure the effective distribution of humanitarian aid in the case of a disaster.

6.4. Regional Aquaculture Potential and How we Can Become a Net Global Supplier

Fish is among the top 10 commodities with potential agri-food value chains in the CARICOM Region. CARICOM's extra-regional imports of fish (fresh, canned, salted) amount to approximately US$72 million (51,000 metric tonnes). Internationally, shrimp and prawns, historically, have been some of the most traded aquatic commodities. In 2021, global exports of shrimp amounted to US$22.2 billion.

The demand for prawns, brackish water shrimp, and inland fish species is growing, and Guyana is poised to tap into these markets while at the same time adding to our export capacity. To be a net global supplier, the government is creating an enabling environment in the following areas:

- **Investment Incentives**: This includes removal of all import duty and tax on fishing vessels, feedstock, pond equipment, and even on

Cage installed for fishing in Pomeroon-Supenaam, Guyana.

fish/seafood processing equipment, packaging material, and other inputs for processing.
- **Regulatory Framework**: This is being developed to advance aquaculture.

In Guyana, investment in aquaculture production capacity supplements marine catches and meets the growing demands in CARICOM and North American markets. The following aquaculture projects are being undertaken in Guyana:

1. Brackish water Shrimp Project;
2. Vannamei Shrimp Project;
3. Cage Fishing.

6.5. Future of Horticulture and Livestock in Guyana

Guyana's horticulture and livestock sectors are growing and have great potential for expansion. The government is actively supporting the development of these sectors and promoting the adoption of modern and sustainable agriculture practices to enhance competitiveness and increase production.

Shade House in Mon Repos.

6.5.1. Horticulture

The demand for fresh fruits and vegetables is growing domestically and internationally, leading the government to launch the Agriculture and Innovation Entrepreneurship Programme in 2022, establishing over 60 shade houses to cultivate high-value crops (carrots, broccoli, cauliflower, etc.).

Further, to enhance the competitiveness of the sector, the government is supporting the development of post-harvest management practices such as proper packaging, grading, and labelling of products and ensuring that food safety and quality standards are met.

Guyana has also focused heavily on promoting sustainable agriculture practices, reducing pesticide use, and promoting organic farming.

6.5.2. Livestock

Guyana continues to invest in producing meat such as lamb, poultry products, milk, and milk products for domestic consumption and export. The country's savannahs are conducive for medium- to large-scale cattle-raising. While milk is already being produced in Guyana, milk and milk products are still the single most imported food group. In 2021, this product accounted for US$45 million (International Trade Centre (ITC)). Therefore, there is a drive to promote the adoption of improved livestock

Improve sheep breed (Dorper).

breeds and modern dairy farming practices, specifically targeting increased productivity and reducing the country's dependence on milk imports.

The government has invested significantly in improving abattoirs and laboratories, genetic material (access to genetic material, embryo transfer, research, and training), and pasture development.

6.6. Investment in Agro-processing

Most of the food in our supermarkets and open markets come from numerous countries. In 2021, the CARICOM Region imported approximately US$1.5 billion of highly processed food, including commodities, such as sweet biscuits, sweetened beverages, sausages, cakes, pastries, and prepared potatoes. Many of these products can be produced locally.

Realizing the untapped potential of this industry, the government has been investing in establishing agro-processing facilities across the country. Thus far, 11 facilities have been established in regions 1, 2, 3, 4, 5, 9, and 10.

Developing the agro-processing industry will reduce the region's food import bill and enhance our agro-processors' livelihood.

Guyanese farm-based products on the market.

6.7. Low Carbon Development Strategy

The Low Carbon Development Strategy (LCDS), Guyana's blueprint of an inclusive and sustainable development strategy, identifies the pathway through which the country could preserve its forest while at the same time growing its economy five-fold over the next 10 years (LCDS 2030). Among other things, the LCDS intends to protect Guyana against climate-related events and biodiversity loss through the promotion of resilient agriculture. Specifically, emphasis will be placed on increasing, among others, the domestic production of agro-processing capabilities, the removal of barriers to intra-regional trade, supporting agri-businesses, smart cultivation, and aquaculture.

The LCDS puts forward four pillars or main objectives towards 2030 and beyond. The first is creating new incentives for our low-carbon economy. Within this objective, the traditional sectors of forestry, mining, and forest-climate service are addressed. It is expanded to also include biodiversity and integrated water resource management, which also addresses marine and ocean economy.

Secondly, the LCDS 2030 also covers plans for adaptation by protecting against climate change and biodiversity loss. The objective focused on aspects that realize climate-resilient agriculture, coastal infrastructure, the protection of mangroves, and climate risk assessment and insurance. These measures build resilience by reducing the risk or severity of climate-related shocks to our food system.

The third objective of the LCDS 2030 is to stimulate future growth through clean energy and low-carbon development. In this pillar, the energy transition with the clean and renewable energy mix is closely examined to decarbonising by 2041 and beyond. In this area, ICT and small & micro-enterprise development are reviewed to assess how we can best build on these pillars to create livelihood and more resilient opportunities that uphold the human rights of our people.

The final objective of the LCDS 2030 looks at aligning national efforts with those climate and biodiversity goals. This is important as we can now integrate each pillar/objective of the LCDS into the other and, by extension, give a holistic yet synergetic view of how we approach our development in a sustainable yet humanly enriching way.

The LCDS 2030 further aligns Guyana with the 2030 Sustainable Development Goals (SDGs) Agenda and the Paris Agreement on climate change. The LCDS 2030 outlines ambitious adaptation and mitigation measures that would see inclusivity, equity for all, and respect for our environment and communities.

6.8. Agriculture Tourism, IWRM, and Land Tenure

The Caribbean Region has some of the most tourism-dependent countries. The growth trajectory for travel and tourism GDP in the Caribbean is forecasted to increase at an average annual rate of 5.5%, more than double the overall economic growth of 2.4% (WTTC, 2022).

This is an indication that the diversification into agri-tourism can be explored once there is the necessary policy support. Additionally, since the agriculture sector is the other pillar upon which the agri-tourism industry will be formed, resilient and sustainable agriculture sectors are equally essential for the industry's development.

As it is, there are varying levels of intersectoral linkages between agriculture and tourism in the Caribbean Region. The Inter-American Institute for Cooperation on Agriculture (IICA) can act as a catalyst to drive the process.

As agri-tourism continues to develop, there is a need for strategic policies and interventions to help develop and stimulate the growth of the industry.

6.8.1. *Policy recommendations*

The key policy recommendations are as follows:

1. creating an enabling policy environment via an agri-tourism policy and roadmap;
2. improving agricultural productivity;

3. promoting agri-tourism and its value chains through strategic investments and public partnerships;
4. strengthening intra-regional collaboration at the multi-national level and between public and private sectors for more impactful multi-destination marketing strategies to promote the uniqueness of the Caribbean brand;
5. investing in improved national rural infrastructure (physical and digital) and regional transportation solutions;
6. developing training, reskilling, and upskilling programmes to equip individuals with the skills required to operate in the agri-tourism industry.

It is incumbent on the leadership of the region to explore policy options that will sustain our quest for food security. In this context, I suggest the following options:

1. We urgently need to address the issue of water for agriculture/food production through the development of a roadmap for **Integrated**

Guyana is home to 18 million hectares of pristine tropical rain forest.

Water Resources Management (IWRM) for each country in the Caribbean.
2. We need to embark on an aggressive **land tenure administration** that provides security of tenure to our farmers and collateral for financial investment in agriculture.
3. We need to explore the options of land banking for food production especially where arable state lands are diminishing.
4. In this age of information technology, we need to design and develop a computerized system for **integrated land resources management** that could minimize the issue of overlapping jurisdiction and conflicts in land use.

Bibliography

Abdib. (2020). Blue Book Infrastructure: A Radiography of Infrastructure Projects in Brazil. 13th February 2023. https://www.abdib.org.br/wp-content/uploads/2021/05/BLUEBOOK_INFRASTRUCTURE.pdf.

Aneja, S. and Lalvani, J. (2021). Role of the private sector and technology for future-ready education and training. In Ra, S., Jagannathan, S., and Maclean, R. (Eds.), *Powering a Learning Society During an Age of Disruption, Education in the Asia-Pacific Region: Issues, Concerns and Prospects*. Springer Nature, Singapore, pp. 293–309. 13th February 2023. https://doi.org/10.1007/978-981-16-0983-1_20.

Beckford, C.L. (2012). Issues in Caribbean food security: Building capacity in local food production systems. 12th February 2023. https://www.researchgate.net/publication/221922784_Issues_in_Caribbean_Food_Security_Building_Capacity_in_Local_Food_Production_Systems.

Behnassi, M. and El Haiba, M. (2022). Implications of the Russia–Ukraine war for global food security. *Nature Human Behaviour*, 6, 754–755. 13th February 2023. https://doi.org/10.1038/s41562-022-01391-x.

Boz, E., Goldfajn, I., Guajardo, J., and Hadzi-Vaskov, M. (2022). Smaller economies in Latin America and Caribbean face a bigger inflation challenge. 13th February 2023. https://www.imf.org/en/News/Articles/2022/09/16/CF-Smaller-Economies-in-Latin-America-and-Caribbean-Face-a-Bigger-Inflation-Challenge.

Caner, M., Grennes, T., and Koehler-Geib, F. (2010). Finding the tipping point — when sovereign debt turns bad. Policy Research Working Paper Series 5391, The World Bank.

Caribbean Agri-Business. (2020). In Antigua & Barbuda — Caribbean agri-business. 12th February 2023. http://agricarib.wmacwebsolutions.comantigua-barbuda-2/.

Caribbean Agri-Business. (2020). In Antigua & Barbuda — Caribbean agri-business. 12th February 2023. http://agricarib.wmacwebsolutions.com/antigua-barbuda-2/.

Caribbean Agribusiness. (2020). Jamaica. 12th February 2023. https://agricarib.org/jamaica-2/.

Caribbean Agribusiness. (2020). Saint Vincent & The Grenadines. 13th February 2023. http://agricarib.wmacwebsolutions.com/saint-vincent-the-grenadines-2/.

Caribbean Agribusiness. (2020). St. Kitts & Nevis — Caribbean agri-business. 13th February 2023. https://agricarib.org/st-kitts-nevis-2/.

Caribbean Agribusiness. (2022). Trinidad & Tobago. 13th February 2023. http://agricarib.wmacwebsolutions.com/trinidad-tobago-2/.

Caribbean Agribusiness. (2022a). Saint Vincent & The Grenadines — Caribbean agri-business. 13th February 2023. http://agricarib.wmacwebsolutions.com/saint-vincent-the-grenadines-2/.

Caribbean Agribusiness. (2022b). Suriname — Caribbean agri-business. 13th February 2023. http://agricarib.wmacwebsolutions.com/suriname-2/.

Caribbean Agribusiness. (2022c). Trinidad & Tobago: Caribbean agri-business. 13th February 2023. http://agricarib.wmacwebsolutions.com/trinidad-tobago-2/.

Caribbean Agricultural Research and Development Institute. (2018). Strategic Plan 2018–2022 Building a Productive and Resilient Regional Agriculture Sector. 12th February 2023. https://www.cardi.org/wp-content/uploads/downloads/2018/05/CARDI-Strategic-Plan-2018-to-2022-Final.pdf.

Caribbean Agricultural Research and Development Institute. (2019). Country profile. 12th February 2023. https://www.cardi.org/country-offices/dominica/.

Caricom Today. (2022). US$7.5B investment required in agriculture-CARICOM business. 12th February 2023. https://today.caricom.org/2022/05/23/us7-5b-investment-required-in-agriculture-caricom-business/.

Caricom Today. (2022a). US$7.5B investment required in agriculture-CARICOM business. *CARICOM Today*. 13th February 2023. https://today.caricom.org/2022/05/23/us7-5b-investment-required-in-agriculture-caricom-business/.

Caricom Today. (2022b). St. Kitts and Nevis fully committed to CARICOM's 25 by 25 agenda to reduce regional food bill. *CARICOM Today*. 13th February 2023. https://today.caricom.org/2022/12/16/st-kitts-and-nevis-fully-committed-to-caricoms-25- by-25-agenda-to-reduce-regional-food-bill/.

Central Statistical Office. (2022). Agriculture statistics. 13th February 2023. https://cso.gov.tt/subjects/agriculture/.

Clapp, J., Moseley, W.G., Burlingame, B., and Termine, P. (2022). Viewpoint: The case for a six-dimensional food security framework. *Food Policy*, 106, 102164. https://doi.org/10.1016/j.foodpol.2021.102164.

Commonwealth of the Bahamas. (2020). U.S. Country Commercial Guides. 12th February 2023. https://www.export-u.com/CCGs/2020/Bahamas-2020-CCG.pdf.

Connell, J. (2014). Food security in the island Pacific: Is Micronesia as far away as ever? *Regional Environmental Change*. 12th February 2023. https://doi.org/10.1007/s10113-014-0696-7.

Constance, C. (2021). High time for resilient agriculture and food systems in St. Vincent and the Grenadines. 13th February 2023. https://ruaf.org/news/high-time-for-resilient-agriculture-and-food-systems-in-st-vincent-and-the-grenadines/.

Cooper, B., Christopher, W., Fernandez, J., Francis, S., Joseph, A., Kentish, R., and Thibou, A. (2015). Forestry Division Antigua & Barbuda's 2015-2020 National Action Plan: Combatting Desertification, Land Degradation & Drought. 12th February 2023. https://info.undp.org/docs/pdc/Documents/ATG/NAP%202015-20%20ANU.pdf.

Crop Trust. (2023). Trinidad & Tobago. 13th February 2023. https://www.croptrust.org/pgrfa-hub/crops-countries-and-genebanks/countries/trinidad-tobago/.

Dame, M.C.W. and University of Notre Dame. (2023). Rankings. Notre Dame Global Adaptation Initiative. University of Notre Dame. 13th February 2023. https://gain.nd.edu/our-work/country-index/rankings/.

De Salvo, C.P. and Anglade, B. (2021). Future foodscapes, a changing landscape in the Haitian agricultural sector. Sostenibilidad. 13th February 2023. https://blogs.iadb.org/sostenibilidad/en/future-foodscapes-a-changing-landscape-in-the-haitian-agricultural-sector/.

Deyal, Z., Giles Álvarez, L., and Waithe, K. (2019). Economic Growth, Debt, and Fiscal Adjustment: Barbados' Tripartite Challenge. Inter-American Development Bank. 13th February 2023. https://doi.org/10.18235/0001563.

Ewing-Chow, D. (2021). Food insecurity in Jamaica doubled projections in 2020. *Forbes*. 13th February 2023. https://www.forbes.com/sites/daphneewingchow/2021/01/24/food-insecurity-in-jamaica-doubled-expectations-in-2020/.

FAO. (2009). Declaration of the world summit on food security. 13th February 2023. https://www.fao.org/fileadmin/templates/wsfs/Summit/Docs/Declaration/WSFS09_Draft_Declaration.pdf.

FAO. (2020). Regional Overview of Food Security in Latin America and the Caribbean.
FAO. (2022). Regional Overview Food Security and Nutrition in Latin America and the Caribbean. 13th February 2023. https://reliefweb.int/report/world/regional-overview-food-security-and-nutrition-latin-america-and-caribbean-towards-improving-affordability-healthy-diets#:~:text=The%20new%20United%20Nations%20report,in%20South%20America%2C%202018.4%25.
FAO. (2022a). The world is at a critical juncture. SDG2 Advocacy Hub. 13th February 2023. https://sdg2advocacyhub.org/news/world-critical-juncture.
FAO. (2022b). The State of Food Security and Nutrition in the World 2021. 13th February 2023. https://doi.org/10.4060/CB4474EN.
FAO. (2023). Home. Science, Technology, and Innovation. Food and Agriculture Organization of the United Nations. 13th February 2023. http://www.fao.org/science-technology-and-innovation/en.
FAOSTAT. (2022). FAOSTAT. 13th February. https://www.fao.org/faostat/en/#data/QV.
Food and Agriculture Organization of the United Nations. (2023). Catastrophic hunger levels recorded for the first time in Haiti. 12th February 2023. https://www.fao.org/newsroom/detail/catastrophic-hunger-levels-recorded-for-the-first-time-in-.
Food and Agriculture Organization, International Fund for Agricultural Development, United Nations Children's Fund, The World Food Programme and Pan American Health Organization. (2023). Regional Overview of Food Security and Nutrition in Latin America and the Caribbean. 12th February 2023. https://www.fao.org/3/cc3859en/cc3859en.pdf.
Food and Agriculture Organization. (2013). Climate Change and Agriculture in Jamaica Agriculture Sector Support Analysis. 12th February 2023. https://www.uncclearn.org/wp-content/uploads/library/fao193.pdf.
Ganpat, W. (2014). *Impacts of Climate Change on Food Security in Small Island Developing States*. IGI Global. Hershey, PA. 13th February 2023. https://www.igi-global.com/book/impacts-climate-change-food-security/108332.
Global Food Security Index. (2022). Economist Impact. 13th February 2023. https://impact.economist.com/sustainability/project/food-security-index/reports/Economist_Impact_GFSI_2022_Global_Report_Sep_2022.pdf.
Government of Saint Lucia. (2013). The Food and Agriculture Organization. 12th February 2023. https://extranet.who.int/nutrition/gina/sites/default/filesstore/LCA%202013%20Food%20nutrition%20security%20action%20plan.pdf.
Government of Saint Lucia. (2018). Saint Lucia's Sectoral Adaptation Strategy and Action Plan for the Agriculture Sector (Agriculture SASAP) 2018-2028.

12th February 2023. https://www4.unfccc.int/sites/NAPC/Documents/Parties/Saint%20Lucia%E2%80%99s%20Sectoral%20Strategy%20and%20Action%20Plan%20for%20Agriculture.pdf.

Green Climate Fund (GCF). (2020). Improving the capacity of the Ministry of Agriculture of Suriname to build resilience to climate change in the agriculture sector. 13th February 2023. https://www.greenclimate.fund/document/improving-capacity-ministry-agriculture-suriname-build-resilience-climate-change.

GRFC. (2022). Global Report on Food Crises 2022 Mid-Year Update — World. ReliefWeb. 13 February 2023. https://reliefweb.int/report/world/global-report-food-crises-2022-mid-year-update.

Hanedar, E., Hong, G.H., Thevenot, C., and Amaglobeli, D. (n.d.). Fiscal Policy for Mitigating the Social Impact of High Energy and Food Prices. 13 February 2023. https://www.imf.org/en/Publications/IMF-Notes/Issues/2022/06/07/Fiscal-Policy-for-Mitigating-the-Social-Impact-of-High-Energy-and-Food-Prices-519013.

IDB. (2018). Agricultural Policy Reports. 13th February 23. https://publications.iadb.org/publications/english/viewer/Analysis-of-Agricultural-Policies-in-Trinidad-and-Tobago.pdf.

IDB. (2018). *Analysis of Agricultural Policies in Trinidad and Tobago*. 13th February 2023. https://www.researchgate.net/publication/325031676_Analysis_of_Agricultural_Policies_in_Trinidad_and_Tobago.

IEA. (2022). How the energy crisis is exacerbating the food crisis — Analysis. 13th February 2023. https://www.iea.org/commentaries/how-the-energy-crisis-is-exacerbating-the-food-crisis.

IFAD. (2021). Haiti. 13th February 2023. https://www.ifad.org/en/web/operations/w/country/haiti.

IICA. (2022). Agriculture in Saint Vincent and the Grenadines has recovered following the volcanic eruptions and the year has begun with exports on the rise. 13th February 2023. https://www.iica.int/en/press/news/agriculture-saint-vincent-and-grenadines-has-recovered-following-volcanic-eruptions-and.

Institute of Belize. (2022). Consumer Prices Rise 5.8% in April 2022: Motor Vehicle Fuels, Food, and LPG Prices Most Affected. 12th February 2023. https://www.belize.org/wp-content/uploads/CPI-April-Release-2022.pdf.

Instituto Interamericano de Cooperacion para la Agricultura. (2019). CROWDFUND IICA COVID-19 Response for the Caribbean. 12th February 2023. https://www.iica.int/themes/custom/iica2019/images/crowfunding/informe_antigua_eng.pdf.

ITA. (2020). Jamaica — Country commercial guide. 12th February 2020. https://www.trade.gov/country-commercial-guides/jamaica-agriculture.

ITA. (2022). Trinidad and Tobago — Agricultural Sectors. International Trade Administration. 13th February 2023. https://www.trade.gov/country-commercial-guides/trinidad-and-tobago-agricultural-sectors.

Kent, P. and Haralambides, H. (2022). A perfect storm or an imperfect supply chain? The U.S. supply chain crisis. *Maritime Economics & Logistics*, 24, 1–8. 13th February 2023. https://doi.org/10.1057/s41278-022-00221-1.

Kogo, B.K., Kumar, L., and Koech, R. (2021). Climate change and variability in Kenya: A review of impacts on agriculture and food security. *Environment, Development and Sustainability*, 23, 23–43. 13th February 2023. https://doi.org/10.1007/s10668-020-00589-1.

Laborde, D., Martin, W., Swinnen, J., and Vos, R. (2020). COVID-19 risks to global food security. *Science*, 369, 500–502. 13th February 2023. https://doi.org/10.1126/science.abc4765.

LCDS. (2021). Guyana's Low Carbon Development Strategy 2030 (Draft for consultation). 13th February 2023. https://lcds.gov.gy/wp-content/uploads/2021/10/LCDS-2030-Final-DRAFT-for-consultation-min.pdf.

Lenderking, H.L., Robinson, S., and Carlson, G. (2021). Climate change and food security in Caribbean small island developing states: Challenges and strategies. *International Journal of Sustainable Development & World Ecology*, 28, 238–245. 13th February 2023. https://doi.org/10.1080/13504509.2020.1804477.

Loop. (2019). St Lucia working with Taiwan to reduce food import bill. 13th February 2023. https://stlucia.loopnews.com/content/st-lucia-working-taiwan-reduce-food-import-bill.

McKinsey. (2022a). The coronavirus effect on global economic sentiment. McKinsey. 13th February 2023. https://www.mckinsey.com/capabilities/strategy-and-corporate-finance/our-insights/the-coronavirus-effect-on-global-economic-sentiment?cid=other-eml-alt-mip-mck&hdpid=7e0ff504-6ddb-426c-b613-b16103730959&hctky=10326800&hlkid=6c8557d4d2d041a4b54725f38b222098.

McKinsey. (2022b). Global food shortage and security: New risks. McKinsey. 13th February 2023. https://www.mckinsey.com/industries/agriculture/our-insights/a-reflection-on-global-food-security-challenges-amid-the-war-in-ukraine-and-the-early-impact-of-climate-change.

MoA. (2022). Guyana investing in reducing the Caricom food import bill 25 by 2025. 13th February 2023. https://agriculture.gov.gy/wp-content/uploads/

2022/07/Guyana-investing-in-reducing-the-Caricom-Food-Import-Bill-25-by-2025.

MoF. (2023). Budget speech 2023. 13th February 2023. https://finance.gov.gy/budget-speech-2023/.

Mohammadi, E., Singh, S.J., McCordic, C., and Pittman, J. (2022). Food security challenges and options in the Caribbean: Insights from a scoping review. *Anthropocene Science*, 1, 91–108. 13th February 2023. https://doi.org/10.1007/s44177-021-00008-8.

ND-GAIN. (2023). Methodology. 12th February 2023. https://gain.nd.edu/our-work/country-index/methodology/#:~:text=vulnerability%20and%20readiness.-,VULNERABILITY,negative%20effects%20of%20climate%20change.

Newsroom. (2021). Guyana imports about 40% of its food; President Ali targets self-sufficiency. *News Room Guyana*. 12th February 2023. https://newsroom.gy/2021/12/07/guyana-imports-about-40-of-its-food-president-ali-targets-self-sufficiency/.

OEC. (2023). Roraima. OEC — The Observatory of Economic Complexity. 12th February 2023. https://oec.world/en/profile/subnational_bra_state/roraima.

OECD. (2022). The impacts and policy implications of Russia's aggression against Ukraine on agricultural markets. 13th February 2023. https://www.oecd-ilibrary.org/docserver/0030a4cd-en.pdf?expires=1676328157&id=id&accname=guest&checksum=9D630E6CA5262A042 3A3F85EDC98F291.

OECS. (2021). OECS CCASAP Country analysis: Resilience to climate change at a glance — Saint Kitts and Nevis. 12th February 2023. https://www.researchgate.net/publication/354323068_OECS_CCASAP_Country_analysis_resilience_to_climate_change_at_a_glance_-_Saint_Kitts_and_Nevis.

Persaud, R.B. 'Human Security', in Allan Collins 'Human Security,' in Alan Collins (ed.), *Contemporary Security Studies*. Oxford University Press, 2019.

Pörtner, H.-O., Roberts, D.C., et al. (2022). Climate Change 2022: Impacts, Adaptation and Vulnerability. Contribution of Working Group II to the Sixth Assessment Report of the Intergovernmental Panel on Climate Change. Cambridge University Press. 13th February 2023. https://www.researchgate.net/profile/Sina-Ayanlade/publication/362431678_Climate_Change_2022_Impacts_Adaptation_and_Vulnerability_Working_Group_II_Contribution_to_the_Sixth_Assessment_Report_of_the_Intergovernmental_Panel_on_Climate_Change/links/62ea52343c0ea87887793180/Climate-Change-2022-

Impacts-Adaptation-and-Vulnerability-Working-Group-II-Contribution-to-the-Sixth-Assessment-Report-of-the-Intergovernmental-Panel-on-Climate-Change.pdf.

Sachs, J., Massa, I., Marinescu, S., and Lafortune, G. (2021). The decade of action and small island developing states: Measuring and addressing SIDS' vulnerabilities to accelerate SDG progress. 13th February 2023. https://irp.cdn-website.com/be6d1d56/files/uploaded/WP_MVI_Sachs%20Massa%20Marinescu%20Lafortune_FINAL_cVeeBVmKSKyYYS6OyiiH.pdf.

Shik, O., Boyce, R.A., Salvo, C.P.D., and Egas, J.J. (2018). Analysis of Agricultural Policies in Trinidad and Tobago. Inter-American Development Bank.

Shultz, J.M., Kossin, J.P., Shepherd, J.M., Ransdell, J.M., Walshe, R., Kelman, I., and Galea, S. (2019). Risks, Health Consequences, and Response Challenges for Small-Island- Based Populations: Observations from the 2017 Atlantic Hurricane Season. *Disaster Medicine and Public Health Preparedness*, 13, 5–17. 12th February 2023. https://doi.org/10.1017/dmp.2018.28.

The Borgen Project. (2020). Hunger in Dominica: 5 fast facts. 12th February 2023. https://borgenproject.org/hunger-in-dominica-facts/.

The Borgen Project. (2021). The Borgen project. Downsize poverty the Borgen project. 13th February 2023. https://borgenproject.org/ (Accessed 30 January 2023).

The Economist. (2022). Progress to eradicate global hunger is stalling. 13th February 2023. https://www.economist.com/graphic-detail/2022/03/09/progress-to-eradicate-global-hunger-is-stalling.

The Economist. (2022). The coming food catastrophe. 13th February 2023. https://www.economist.com/leaders/2022/05/19/the-coming-food-catastrophe.

The Government of Bahamas. (2022). The Bahamas Climate Spending Report 2021–2022. 12th February 2023. https://www.bahamasbudget.gov.bs/media/filer_public/b7/02/b7023716-9201-456e-ac36-524fac35be8a/bahamas_climatespending_2021_22.pdf.

The Government of St. Vincent and the Grenadines. (2011). Country Programme Framework (CPF) 2012–2015 for St. Vincent and the Grenadines Agricultural Sector. 13th February 2023. https://www.fao.org/3/bp528e/bp528e.pdf.

The World Bank Group. (2021). Haiti. 12 February 2023. https://climateknowledgeportal.worldbank.org/country/haiti/vulnerability.

Tidemann, J., Piatkov, V., and Prihardini, D. (2022). *Meeting the Sustainable Development Goals in Small Developing States with Climate Vulnerabilities:*

Cost and Financing. IMF. 13th February 2023. https://statics.teams.cdn.office.net/evergreen-assets/safelinks/1/atp-safelinks.html.

Tietze, F., Vimalnath, P., Aristodemou, L., and Molloy, J. (2022). Crisis-critical intellectual property: Findings from the COVID-19 pandemic. *IEEE Transactions on Engineering Management*, 69, 2039–2056. 12th February 2023. https://doi.org/10.1109/TEM.2020.2996982.

USAID. (2017). Climate risk profile: Jamaica. 12th February 2023. https://www.climatelinks.org/sites/default/files/asset/document/2017_USAID-CCIS_Climate-Risk-Profile-Jamaica.

von Grebmer, K., Bernstein, J., and Reiner, L. (2022). 2022 Global Hunger Index: Food Systems Transformation and Local Governance. Concern Worldwide.

WEF. (2022a). Here's how the food and energy crises are connected. World Economic Forum. 12th February 2023. https://www.weforum.org/agenda/2022/09/heres-how-the-food-and-energy-crises-are-connected/.

WEF. (2022b). The big challenges for supply chains in 2022. World Economic Forum. 12th February 2023. https://www.weforum.org/agenda/2022/01/challenges-supply-chains-covid19-2022/.

WEF. (2022c). Agricultural technology needs public private partnerships. World Economic Forum. 12th February 2023. https://www.weforum.org/agenda/2022/03/unlock-the-power-of-agricultural-technology-through-private-public-partnerships/.

WFP. (2022). A global food crisis. World Food Programme. 12th February 2023. https://www.wfp.org/global-hunger-crisis.

WFP. (2022a). Understanding the Energy Crisis and Its Impact on Food Security (August 2022) — World. ReliefWeb. 12th February 2023. https://reliefweb.int/report/world/understanding-energy-crisis-and-its-impact-food-security-august-2022.

WFP. (2022b). WFP Haiti Country Brief. 13th February 2023. https://docs.wfp.org/api/documents/WFP-0000145510/download/.

WITS. (2020). Suriname food products imports by country 2020. WITS Data. 12th February 2023. https://wits.worldbank.org/CountryProfile/en/Country/SUR/Year/LTST/TradeFlow/Import/Partner/by-country/Product/16-24_FoodProd.

World Bank. (2013). Agriculture in Haiti: Highly vulnerable, mostly uninsured. World Bank. 13th February 2023. https://www.worldbank.org/en/news/feature/2013/04/03/agriculture-in-haiti-highly-vulnerable-mostly-uninsured (Accessed 17 January 23).

World Bank. (2018). World Bank provides US$65 million for Dominica's Post-Maria reconstruction. 13th February 2023. https://www.worldbank.org/en/

news/press-release/2018/04/13/world-bank-provides-us65-million-for-dominicas-post-maria-reconstruction.

World Bank. (2020). Nutrition Smart Agriculture in Haiti. 11th February 2023. https://documents1.worldbank.org/curated/en/222031597126417223/pdf/Nutrition-Smart-Agriculture-in-Haiti.pdf.

World Bank. (2022). The World Bank in Haiti. 12th February 2022. https://www.worldbank.org/en/country/haiti/overview.

World Bank. (2022a). Food security. Rising food insecurity in 2022. World Bank. 13th February 2023. https://www.worldbank.org/en/topic/agriculture/brief/food-security-update (Accessed 11 January 23).

World Bank. (2022b). Food insecurity in the Caribbean. World Bank. 13th February 2023. https://www.worldbank.org/en/news/feature/2022/06/28/food-insecurity-caribbean (Accessed 18 January 23).

World Bank. (2023). Agriculture, forestry, and fishing, value added (% Of GDP)–Dominica. 12th February 2023. https://data.worldbank.org/indicator/NV.AGR.TOTL.ZS?locations=DM.

World Bank. (2023). St. Lucia. 12th February 2023. https://data.worldbank.org/country/LC.

World Bank. (2023). The World Bank in Haiti — Overview World Bank. 13th February 2023. https://www.worldbank.org/en/country/haiti/overview.

World Economic Forum. (2022). How can we protect food systems against global shocks? Here's what business leaders say, World Economic Forum. 13th February 2023. https://www.weforum.org/agenda/2022/05/protect-food-systems-against-global-shocks/.

Name Index

Acharya, A., xxi, xxii
Ali, Arya, 88
Ali, Mohamed Irfaan, xiv, xxi
Aneja, S., 89
Anglade, B., 52, 53
Aristodemou, L., 7

Beckford, C.L., 12, 54
Behnassi, M., 5, 6
Bernstein, J., 3, 4
Boyce, R.A., 79
Boz, E, 18
Burlingame, B., 3

Caner, M., 20, 74
Carlson, G., 22
Christopher, W., 24
Clapp, J., 3
Connell, J., 20
Cooper, B., 24

Dame, M.C.W., 20, 55
De Salvo, C.P.,, 52, 53
Deyal, Z., 33
Dongyu, Q., xvi

Egas, J.J., 79
El Haiba, M., 5, 6

Fernandez, J., 24
Francis, S., 24

Galea, S., 22
Ganpat, W.G., 11
Goldfajn, I., 18
Grennes, T., 74
Guajardo, J., 18

Hadzi-Vaskov, M., 18
Haralambides, H., 8

Kelman, I., 22
Kentish, R., 24
Kent, P., 8
Koech, R., 7
Koehler-Geib, F., 74
Kogo, B.K., 7
Kossin, J.P., 22
Kumar, L., 7

Laborde, D., 6
Lafortune, G., 20

Lalvani, J., 89
Lenderking, L.H., 22
Lubetkin, M., xix

Marinescu, S., 20
Martin, W., 6
Massa, I., 20
McCordic, C., 11
Mohammadi, E., 11
Molloy, J., 7
Moseley, W.G., 3
Mottley, M., 84

Piatkov, V, 20
Pittman, J., 11
Pörtner, H.O., 7
Prihardini, D., 20

Ransdell, J.M., 22
Reiner, L., 3, 4
Robinson, S., 22

Sachs, J., 20
Salvo, C.P.D., 79
Shepherd, J.M., 22
Shik, O., 79
Shultz, J.M., 22
Singh, S.J., 11
Swinnen, J., 6

Termine, P., 3
Thibou, A., 24
Tideman, J., 20

Vimalnath, P., 7
von Grebmer, K., 3, 4
Vos, R., 6

Waithe, K., 33
Walshe, R., 22

Subject Index

Africa, xxiv, 4, 6, 7
agriculture, ix, x, xiv–xvi, xxii, xxiii, 2, 3, 8, 11, 15–17, 23, 24, 26–28, 33, 34, 37, 40, 41, 43–46, 48–50, 53–55, 57, 58, 60–62, 65–67, 69, 70, 73, 74–79, 82, 83, 87, 89, 92, 93, 94, 97, 99, 100, 102, 104, 106, 107, 109–112
Agriculture Investment, 82
Agro-processing, 108
Antigua and Barbuda, 11, 20, 23–27, 104
Arable land, 12, 23, 28, 31, 35, 38, 42, 45, 50, 54, 58, 62, 66, 70, 75

Bahamas, 11, 27–29
bananas, 38, 50, 55, 58, 62, 66, 71
Bangalore Bio Innovation Centre, 87
Barbados, 11, 18, 31–33, 84, 102, 103–105
Belize, 34–37
Brazil, 5, 90
BRICS, xxiii, xxiv
Buenos Aires Declaration, xviii

Caribbean, ix–xix, xxiii, xxiv, 4, 7, 11–20, 24, 31, 40, 50, 51, 58, 67, 71, 72, 76, 81–83, 87, 88, 90–92, 94, 97, 98, 100, 104, 110–112
CARICOM, ix, xi, xiii, xviii, xix, 11–13, 16, 18, 19, 21, 48, 64, 82, 93, 94, 97–99, 101, 105, 106, 108
CELAC, ix, xviii
cereals, 18, 52
China, xxi, xxiii
climate change, xiv, xix, xxi, xxiv, 7, 8, 11, 14, 15, 20, 21, 24, 25, 28, 29, 32, 33, 36, 39, 42, 43, 46, 50, 51, 53, 55, 56, 58, 59, 63, 67, 71, 72, 76, 77, 109, 110
coffee, 55, 76, 77
Common External Tariff, 95
corn, 6, 50, 81, 101, 102
COVID-19, xiii–xv, xviii, xxi, 1, 5–7, 12, 14, 18, 30, 33, 40, 53, 61, 72, 81

dairy, 28, 55, 108
debt-to-GDP, 18–20, 23, 26, 33, 40, 43, 45, 48, 53, 54, 57, 61, 62, 65, 66, 69, 75, 79

dependency, 12, 17, 18, 26, 29, 39, 43, 47, 51–53, 55, 59, 64, 68, 72, 76, 77
Dominica, 11, 20, 22, 38–40

e-agriculture, 92, 93
ECLAC, 18
energy crisis, 8, 12
Ethiopia, 6
Europe, xxiv, 5
European Union, 38, 66, 68
exports, xxiii, 5, 6, 62, 66, 68, 71, 76, 77, 95, 105

fertilizer, xvi, 1, 5, 8, 18
fish, 37, 63, 96, 103, 105, 106
Food and Agriculture Organization (FAO), ix, xvi, xviii, xix, xxii, 3
food dependency, 51, 53, 77
food imports, xiii, xiv, 2, 11–13, 16–18, 26, 29–33, 35, 39, 40, 43, 44, 47, 51, 52, 55–57, 59, 60, 64, 68, 69, 72, 73, 76, 78, 83, 91, 92, 98
food insecurity, xiv–xvii, xix, xxiii, xxiv, 1, 4–7, 11, 14, 17, 23, 25–28, 31, 32, 34, 36, 38, 41, 42, 45, 49, 50, 54, 56, 65, 68, 70, 72, 82, 88
food production, xiii–xv, xviii, xix, 7, 8, 11, 14–16, 18, 24–26, 28, 31–33, 35, 36, 39, 40, 42, 46–50, 53, 55–58, 60, 63–65, 67, 68, 71–73, 76–79, 81, 89, 92, 111, 112

GDP *per capita*, 23, 27, 31, 34, 38, 41, 45, 49, 54, 57, 62, 66, 70, 75
Global North, xxii, xxiv

Global South, xxii–xxiv
Grenada, 11, 20, 41–43
Guyana, x–xiv, xxi, 11, 13, 18, 28, 45–49, 82, 85, 89–91, 94, 96, 101–108, 110, 111

Haiti, 11, 13, 14, 18, 20, 49–53
hinterland, 46
Horticulture, 106, 107
human security, xxi, xxii, xxiv, xxv
hunger, xiv–xvii, xix, xxi–xxiii, 1–6, 11, 20, 51, 87–89
hurricanes, 24, 28, 50, 55, 58

imports, 26, 29–33, 35, 39, 40, 43, 44, 47, 51, 52, 55–57, 59, 60, 64, 68, 69, 72, 73, 76–78
India, xxiii, 87
inflation, xv, xviii, 2, 5, 8, 17–19, 23, 28, 31, 34, 36, 38, 42, 45, 49, 54, 58, 62, 66, 70, 72, 75
infrastructure, 40, 51–53, 61, 69, 83, 95, 104, 109, 111
Israel–Hamas conflict, xxi, xxiii

Jamaica, 11, 18, 22, 54–56

landslides, 50, 55, 58
Latin America, ix, x, xv, xvii–xix, 4, 11, 50
Livestock, 7, 24, 28, 31, 35, 38, 42, 45, 46, 50, 54, 58, 62, 66, 71, 75, 103, 106, 107
logistics, xiv, xvi, 7, 5, 81, 92, 97, 105
Low Carbon Development Strategy (LCDS), 108

McKinsey, 5, 8
Millennium Development Goals, 11

non-tariff barrier, 95, 98

oil, 6, 8, 46, 49, 52, 90

Panorama 2022, xvii, xviii
plantains, 50, 62
poultry, 28, 71, 76, 96, 101, 103, 107
poverty, xv, xvii, xviii, 4, 5, 7–9, 14
public debt, 17, 18, 26, 29, 33, 40, 43, 48, 53, 60, 69, 73, 79

RATC, 82, 83, 85, 87–89
regional food hub, xxiv, 104
rice, 46, 71, 76, 79, 104
Roraima, 89–92
Russia–Ukraine War, xxi

Saint Barnabas Accord, 102
Saint Kitts and Nevis, 11, 20, 62–65
Saint Lucia, 11, 13, 20, 57–61
Saint Vincent and the Grenadines, 11, 66–70
shrimp, 105, 106
SIDS, 18, 24
SMEs, 83
South Asia, 7
soybean, 101
SPS, 98, 103
sugar, 31, 46, 52, 76, 77, 90, 96

supply chain, 1, 2, 4, 7, 8, 12, 18, 90, 100
Suriname, 11, 18, 70, 71–74, 104
Sustainable Development Goals (SDGs), xv, xxiii, 6, 110

tourism, 95, 110, 111
transportation, xiv, xxiii, 8, 81, 92, 95, 97, 102, 104, 111
Trinidad and Tobago, 11, 75–77, 79, 104

Ukraine, xv, xviii, xxi, xxiii, 1, 2, 5, 8, 14, 17, 18
UN, xxii, 6, 83, 91
UNDP, xxii

vegetables, 24, 28, 31, 37, 42, 60, 62, 76, 102, 107
vulnerability, 15, 20, 21, 24, 25, 28–30, 32, 33, 36, 39, 42, 43, 46, 47, 50–52, 55, 56, 59, 63, 67, 71, 72, 76, 77

weather, 11, 12, 20, 24, 28, 42, 58, 63
WHO, 9
World Bank, 2, 12–15, 17–20, 24–26, 28–33, 35, 36, 38–40, 42, 44–47, 50–54, 56–60, 62–64, 66–68, 71–73, 75, 77, 78
World Food Programme, 1

Milton Keynes UK
Ingram Content Group UK Ltd.
UKHW050454041224
452022UK00011B/100

9 789811 298899